Sajid Abdul

This is the first piece of fiction by Sajid Abdul, who wants his writing to be remembered with love. When he's not writing novels, Sajid loves to read historical fiction or watch movies and write on topics that interest him.

Connect with him on Instagram @sajiddd.__ for updates on his works.

English Language
Face-Off @ the Reunion
(Novel)
by
Sajid Abdul
♦
Published in December 2024
By SMS Publications
E-Mail : Publicationssms@gmail.com

♦
Cover Design
Mehrin Nisa
♦
Printed at
Repro India Ltd.

ISBN 978-93-3418-185-2

FACE-OFF
@the Reunion

Sajid Abdul

This novel is a work of fiction. Names, characters, places, incidents and dialogues are either the product of the author's imagination or are used fictitiously. Any resemblance to actual events, locales, organizations, or persons, living or dead, is entirely coincidental and beyond the intent of the author.

Acknowledgements

I thank my wife & children for their support and boost without which I would never have been able to complete this book.

A special thanks to friends who encouraged me in this mission.

Preface

This book is an ode to my beloved city Cuttack — the Millennium City. A city where the pulse of life beats in harmony with tradition, culture, and an unyielding spirit of unity. Cuttack is not just a place on the map; it is a vibrant essence of all that defines communal harmony, where the flavor of different religions and traditions blends into a beautiful symphony, especially during its festivals.

It's the same place where I spent countless days hanging out with my school friends, wandering through its streets and living through the magical moments of our teenage years. Those carefree days, filled with laughter and adventure, are etched in my memory like golden treasures —reminders of a time when life was simple, and the bond of friendship was sheer joy.

The city's soul lay, or still lies, in its famous khatti, a ritual coming together of friends to sit and unburden their hearts, gossip to their hearts' content, exchanging stories, laughter, and dreams. And no homage to Cuttack will be complete without a salute to its iconic street food, especially Dahibara aludam and Lassi sharbat, a culinary anthem that stirs nostalgia and love in the hearts of all who've savored its flavors.

Cuttack rests along the serene banks of the mighty Mahanadi, offering a perfect balance of tranquility and vibrancy. This city, with its rich tapestry of history, culture, and warmth, has shaped me, inspired me, and will forever hold a special place in my heart. This book is a tribute to you, Cuttack — with gratitude, respect, and endless love.

Introduction to the Book

In a world that once thrived on handwritten letters, where landlines were lifelines and friendships were nurtured in the warmth of face-to-face laughter, a group of schoolmates once ruled the corridors of their alma mater. Back then, in the'90s, there were no buzzing phones to interrupt conversations, no glowing screens to steal glances at dinner tables, and no social media apps begging for likes or comments. Life unfolded between the pages of Tintin comics, DC comics, Hardy Boys, Nancy Drew, and Archie's — their adventures lived through books, journals, and the thrilling crackle of VHS tapes. Those were the days of real excitement, a time when adventure felt alive compared to the digital haze of today's world. Their universe was simple —friends, families, love for nature and the unfiltered joy of being together.

But times changed.

Two decades had passed since they last walked those halls together, now scattered across different cities, countries, and lives. They had evolved with the times, embracing the digital age that brought them closer yet kept them apart. Until one day, a single notification lit up their Facebook feeds — a post in their long-forgotten group.

The message was brief but electrifying: "Let's meet. December 26, 2014. Same place, same faces. Time to catch up."

For the first time in years, they all paused. The inseparable gang that had grown up in a time of laughter, drama, and the kind of love that only youth could spark, now had a chance to reunite. A chance to face each other, not through screens or status updates, but in the flesh — complete with stories, laughter, heartbreak, and the bittersweet reminder of what once was. What would happen when their worlds collided? Could they rekindle the magic, or had the years and the digital distance transformed them beyond recognition?

It had been ages since the corridors of Centurion School echoed with their laughter, but the memories never faded. Life had moved on, yet something in their hearts still lingered, tethered to the innocence of their school days. In the era of Facebook and fleeting digital connections, a spark was ignited among the long-lost classmates when they stumbled upon the 'School Friends Reunion' group. What began as casual chats filled with nostalgia quickly turned into a serious plan — a reunion.

After months of debate, they finally settled on a date on a chilly winter's day in Cuttack, a city in the Eastern state of Odisha, India. It was decided they would meet at the place where it all began — their old school, Centurion, nestled between ancient trees and streets that had witnessed countless moments of their youth. For many, it would be the first time since decades that they would step foot in the school, let alone see each other.

Sameer, the story's main protagonist, was no different. He had lived many lives since his school days — a family man, a professional, a traveler — but there was something magical about this reunion that pulled him back to a time he had tucked away in the far corners of his mind. As he journeyed back, excitement brewed within him, mixed with a touch of nervous anticipation. Old faces, old stories, and long-buried emotions awaited him.

As the sun rose on that fateful December morning, Sameer found himself back in familiar territory. With every step he took toward the school gate, a flood of memories washed over him. Friends whom he hadn't seen in years, now stood before him, older yet filled with the same youthful energy that once bound them together.

Throughout the day, Sameer relived moment after moment — funny incidents, teenage heartbreaks, mischief in class, and those secretive crushes. The reunion was not just about catching up; it was about reopening the chapters of their collective past. As the sun set and night crept in, the gathering transformed into a celebration of the past and the present.

It was more than just a date — it was a chance to reconnect, to relive the days before social media ruled their lives, and to remember what it felt like to truly be with one another. Little did they know, this reunion would be much more than just a nostalgic trip down memory lane — it would become a rediscovery of old flames, forgotten rivalries, and the timeless bond that only childhood friends could share.

The reunion was set. The countdown had begun.

What followed would be an unforgettable face-off — an event bursting with fun, laughter, drama, love, and emotions only a reunion could unleash through the eyes of Sameer.

"The moment had arrived — the confrontation between past and present was about to unfold."

Mission Reunion plan on Facebook

Facebook Group Forum: School Friends Reunion
Date: April 30, 2014

Tanya
April 30, 2014 - 10:32 AM

Hey Guys & Girls, Sameer and I were discussing this the other day and came up with this idea...why don't we plan something big and nice this December....I know this is quite an advanced planning...but this is just to ensure that all our friends staying away from home and India get enough time to plan their vacations accordingly. Sometime between 25thDec and 1stJan would be a good time, considering the holiday time for us and kids and hopefully less hectic work at office too.... Thoughts??

20 LIKES

Arun
April 30, 2014 - 11:01 AM

Wow! Happy Birthday Tanya……It sounds really great! Are the girls in!!! Thanks, FB, for giving me an opportunity to see them all once again.

25 LIKES

Sanjay
April 30, 2014 - 11:15 AM

Hey Tanya Happy Birthday! …. I'm in, just let me know when and where…. thanks to FB.

10 LIKES

Kavya

April 30, 2014 - 11:45 AM

Happy Birthday, Tanya! And what a great idea. Let's seriously plan a get-together—thanks to FB, at least we are in touch! Let me check with Komal, Rebecca, Meera, and the others to see if they'll join us.

15 LIKES

Sameer

April 30, 2014 - 12:05 PM

Hey Tanya, Happy Birthday once again—finally you aged…just kidding! Enjoy and have a blast.

Wake up, gang! The school bell rings again…it's time for action for the DRDA boys after almost 20 years. Diamond Rodney Detective Agency, who shocked everyone with our mystery-solving skills, is ready to roll…hope Priya is around. This is a mind-blowing idea, and I'm ready to rock again with all of you. Let's recreate the magic once more! "Hip Hip Hurray"!

Thanks, FB, for uniting us all—love you.

40 LIKES

Sanjay

April 30, 2014 - 12:30 PM

Nuts! I'm sick and bored of this bloody office and my nagging boss. My life sucks in this atmosphere—I seriously need a break. Target! Target! Target! The month never ends. It feels like I'm made for sales and married to this organization.

Hey Sameer, plan it up. I know you can do it, Sameer — "Hey Tanya, Happy Birthday! Where's the party tonight?" Call us—I'm sure we'll rock it once again.

What say, gang? Let's surprise Tanya and rock the floor. Phew! Sorry, I forgot we're all in different places now... It's a dream to be together again. But hey boy, only you can make it happen. Think fast. But thanks FB for giving me back my friends.

30 LIKES

Rebecca

April 30, 2014 - 1:00 PM

I have one condition, let it not be a wine party, as the boys get crazy, and we end up spoiling the mood. Let's keep it interactive and interesting since we haven't seen each other in ages.

25 LIKES

Sameer

April 30, 2014 - 1:15 PM

I'm okay with it, gang, as long as we enjoy each other's company within our comfort zones.

10 LIKES

Private Message between Arun and Sameer

Arun's Personal Message

April 30, 2014 - 2:00 PM

Dude! How did you agree to their condition of no booze? That's ridiculous! I can't do it without drinks…work something out and let me know. I'm curious to hear back from you.

Sameer's Reply to Arun

April 30, 2014 - 2:30 PM

I get it, man! Don't worry—we'll see what we can do without stirring up too much drama. We'll make sure it's fun for everyone.

Private Message between Tanya and Sameer

Tanya's Personal Message

April 30, 2014 - 3:00 PM

Sameer, just let me know if the reunion will be a family get together or just the batch? I need to plan accordingly. Bye, take care.

Sameer's Reply to Tanya

April 30, 2014 - 3:20 PM

Tanya, does it really matter whether it's a family thing or just a group reunion? Either way is fine—my wife's cool with coming along. Let's just get this reunion going first, and we can sort out the rest later.

Private Message between Rebecca and Sameer.

Rebecca's Personal Message

April 30, 2014 - 4:00 PM

Sameer, everyone's in, but most of us think it's better if we don't include families. It just feels a bit odd, and some are skeptical about how their spouses would react to old friends. What do you think?

Sameer's Reply to Rebecca

April 30, 2014 - 4:15 PM that's fine, Rebecca. If everyone's more comfortable with it being just the school group, I'm okay with it. Let's move forward with the reunion!

After few months on August 30 2014.

In the dim glow of our screens, the group chat buzzed with tension later Arguments flew, each friend stubbornly holding onto their own preferred date.

"December's impossible for me!" typed Arun, exasperated.

"I can't do January either," Rebecca fired back.

"My year ending closing guys' added Sanjay.

"Look, this is getting nowhere," Sameer finally cuts in, his fingers trembling slightly. "We've been talking for months. It's now or never."

A brief silence fell over the chat.

"Fine," Tanya chimed in, breaking the stillness. "December 26th. Let's just make it happen. "One by one, reluctant but resigned, the messages echoed through: Agreed. December 26th.

30 LIKES.

I leaned back, my heart racing. It was done. The reunion was set—no turning back now.

December 16, 2014

The journey to India for the reunion

The journey from Dubai to the reunion began, the excitement was palpable, but beneath the surface, my heart raced for reasons beyond a family wedding or a vacation. My mind was consumed by thoughts of the upcoming reunion — a meeting with my old schoolmates after two decades.

The plane hummed as it cruised through the clouds, and my family was already immersed in their own thoughts. Sofia, my wife, was gushing about her brother's wedding, chatting with my daughters Sanya and Sonia, who were equally thrilled to attend the wedding and meet their grandparents and cousins. But my mind was far from the chatter.

Sofia, sitting beside me, had noticed my unusual excitement. She turned to me with a mischievous glint in her eye and asked, "So, what's got you in such a good mood? It's not just the wedding, is it?" I laughed it off, throwing in a quip about the flight attendants to deflect her question. But Sofia wasn't fooled. "Hmm, I think there's more to this trip than just a reunion. Maybe… an old flame?" she whispered; her words laced with playful suspicion.

I felt my heart skip a beat and suddenly it reminded me of Sana, my crush in school. Even after all these years, the mere mention of her name had a strange effect on me. Sofia watched the change in my expression, the blush that crept into my cheeks, and she smiled knowingly.

As the plane's cabin dimmed and passengers drifted into their naps, I found myself sinking into memories of my school days. I had never told Sofia much about Sana, yet she was, teasing me about the one name that still tugged at my heart. My mind wandered back to the halls of my school, where I had first laid my eyes on Sana. She had been the definition of beauty — quiet, intelligent, always lost in a book. I admired her from afar, too shy to ever speak my heart.

But it was that last day of school which haunted me. The plane lights dimmed and my eyes closed and another beam of light took me down memory lane.

Flashback - The Last Day at School

Place- Centurion School Time: 1: 00 pm

Hip! Hip! Hurray! "We are free birds now!" The cheer echoed through the school on the final day. The excitement was palpable as students burst crackers, snapped photos with Sam's prized camera, and celebrated the end of an era. I was tucked away, savoring the moment quietly. It was a bittersweet joy; I was thrilled to be free, yet I also felt a pang of sadness. It was the end of an era, and my heart was heavy with the knowledge that I hadn't mustered the courage to tell Sana how I truly felt.

Sana had been my silent obsession for years. Her smile and her charm captivated me, but I had never found the courage to express my feelings. It wasn't until the romantic blockbuster, Aamir Khan-starrer *QSQT* released in 1988 that I realized what I felt for her was real love — not mere infatuation. Even though my friends always teased me about my feelings, claiming I was obsessed without any dreams of a future, I knew that my love for her was pure and genuine.

While everyone else was celebrating the end of school life, I stood alone, removed from the chaos, a silent observer, taking in the scene with bittersweet nostalgia. The moment was perfect, a fleeting snapshot of unadulterated joy, and I was content to let it wash over me like a gentle wave. That is, until a sudden, stinging slap landed on my back, jolting me out of my reverie. "What are you doing here alone, you sickening fellow?" Suraj's voice boomed behind me, his words dripping with exaggerated drama. "Come on, join us in the group! We're celebrating, not attending a funeral!" Suraj a very close friend, the daredevil of the group, who lived life at full throttle and never backed down from anything. He was the one who could excite the group and make everyone laugh in the face of danger.

Suddenly, Sana emerged from the classroom, hurrying towards the field leading to the school's exit gate. I watched helplessly, with heart sinking and turned to Suraj and asked, "Can you take a picture of her? Just a few snaps, if possible, please". He agreed, rushing over to click a series of photos like a paparazzi despite Sana's visible discomfort. Every click was a stolen treasure, a keepsake of a love that had never been spoken aloud. "Enough," I finally said, my voice barely audible. "That's enough."

Finally, Sam and Jacky arrived, noticing the paparazzi. Sam, the most handsome guy in school, was like everyone's heartthrob, his mere presence enough to make heads turn; his intelligence even astounded teachers at times. He had an aura of invincibility, a Casanova who could charm the coldest heart with a single smile. He was destined for greatness, his name whispered in awe by everyone who crossed his path. He was my best friend in school and with him was another hunk, Jacky.

Jacky was very stylish, a good dancer and a primary member of our gang. Both he and Sam were the talk of the town, particularly among girls of St Peterson girl's school. Sam's sharp eyes caught the sadness on my face. "So, is this the end of your love story?" he asked me.

"Yeah, it seems so," I replied with a sad tone.

Sam, ever the provocateur, nudged me. "If you don't propose today, you might never get another chance. Sana is a brilliant student. She might leave the city for higher studies."

His words struck a chord. I gazed at the sky, feeling the weight of missed opportunities. Jacky, ever the motivator, brought his bike in front of me and said, "Buddy, you need to hurry. She's about to leave."

Sam pushed me towards the bike, urgency written all over his face. "Go! She's moving towards home!" The adventure began on the triple ride on one bike and my heart raced. The thought of proposing to her after all these years was terrifying. I had faced countless exams, but this was different — this was real, uncharted territory. The crowd was maddening on the road and Sana was speeding away in her vehicle. We were trying our best to catch up but were getting stranded in the traffic.

After some time, our bike finally caught up with Sana's vehicle. We slowed down to be close enough to be able to speak. My friends were on the edge, nudging me to express my feelings. But I was lost in her eyes, numbed, while my friends kept shouting, "Say it! Tell her you love her...Come on it's now or never... have you freaked out!" But it was all in vain, as my lips were sealed. I lacked the courage to utter a single word.

The pressure mounted. Sam's impatience and anger reached a peak. "Are you saying it, or should I?" He shouted. With a heavy heart pounding, I finally said, "Fine! You ask her!"

Sam, the Casanova, just blurted out, on my behalf, what I was struggling to put into words.

Looking at her straight, he said, "Sana, Sameer loves you very much. Do you love him?"

My heart was in my throat as I eagerly waited to see what she was going to say. She finally opened her mouth, her lips unveiled the word "No", hitting me like a sledgehammer. Sam, undeterred, asked again, "Are you sure?" She affirmed, "No." Sam asked one last time, "Are you absolutely sure?" Her resolute "No" still echoes in my mind.

And just like that, my world came crashing down. The 'No' reverberated in my mind, louder and louder, until it was all I could hear. My dreams shattered like a glass, and I felt a hollow emptiness settle in the pit of my stomach.

Jacky, sensing my despair, brought the bike to a stop. "Let's go back, man. It's over."

As we rode back to school, I was heartbroken. The joy, the hope, the excitement — it was all gone, replaced by a deep, aching sadness. I had lost her, not to someone else, but to my own fear and hesitation.

That day, a part of me died. The part that believed in fairy tales, in happy endings, in the magic of first love. But as we walked back through the school gates, the echoes of my friends' laughter ringing in my ears, I realized something else. Life goes on.

Finally, the plane landed at the destination and I was awakened back to my senses for the reunion.

The Face-off with a Daredevil ride

Location - Cuttack city

As I rolled into my hometown after what felt like an eternity, the streets seemed both familiar and alien, like a dream where everything is recognizable but just a little... different. The sky above was an ominous mix of nostalgia and impending rain, and as I turned onto the riverside road, I inhaled the unmistakable smells of the river – a cocktail of mud, algae, and youthful recklessness – yanking me straight into the past.

It was the riverbank, that sacred stretch of chaos where we lived like invincible kings. Back during our school days, my friends and I had our own personal Grand Prix. We'd hop on a single, battered old bike, triple riding like legends, as if traffic laws were mere suggestions and helmets were for people without a sense of adventure. Daylight wasn't a warning; it was an invitation. We'd roar down that ring road like a pack of wild hyenas, engines screaming as we zigzagged through the narrow lanes, the wind slapping our faces, daring us to go faster.

Nothing would stop us. Well, almost nothing. In the early 1990s the Mandal Commission was formed to address social and educational backwardness in India, and when the government planned to implement its suggestions, to reserve seats in educational institutions and jobs for those who had been left behind, it sparked a major political and societal upheaval. There were widespread protests, particularly from students and people from the upper castes, who saw it as unfair. These protests escalated into violent agitations, with tragic incidents of self-immolation by students. Despite the intense opposition, the policy marked a turning point in addressing historical inequalities, reshaping Indian politics by mobilizing caste-based movements and altering the electoral landscape

In many places, schools and colleges were closed, public transport was disrupted, and clashes between protestors and police were common. One of the most tragic outcomes of the agitations was a wave of self-immolations by students, with several young protestors setting themselves on fire to oppose the reservations.

The curfews and violence marked a turbulent period in Indian history, highlighting the deep societal divisions over caste-based affirmative action and the long-standing issue of social inequality.

It was a strange, quiet time when the whole world seemed to have pressed a pause button. Curfew was in place at many places, and people were stuck indoors for a few days. The streets outside were eerily silent, like the calm before a storm. There were no mobile phones those days to check, no social media apps buzzing with notifications —just landlines, those big clunky things with rotary dials, long twisting cords that always seemed to end up in knots no matter how carefully you handled them.

Suraj, my partner-in-crime, called one afternoon. It was just after lunch, and we were immediately lost in conversation. We talked about everything — from our latest, half-baked mischievous plans to the latest cricket match. We forgot how long we had spoken until I heard my mother calling out from the other room, sounding slightly annoyed. "There are other people in the house who are expecting calls, you know! Disconnect the line!"

Grudgingly, we hung up, but we weren't done talking yet. Not by a long shot. We'd sneak onto the other parallel lines in our homes — those extra phones connected to the same landline — and continue talking as if no one had interrupted us. It was our secret trick, a way to keep the conversation going without raising suspicion. Well, not too much suspicion, anyway.

There was always something crazy to talk about. Sometimes, Suraj would spin ridiculous plans, like taking his dad's scooter out for a late-night spin, or we'd plot an imaginary escape from the monotony of lockdown. But the real thrill came when I'd get calls from my friends' girlfriends, all carefully timed and coded. Their requests were usually simple: "Can you tell him to call at 7 pm? My parents will be watching TV by then." Parental vigilance was a real obstacle, and landline phones made clandestine teenage romances that much harder to manage.

I remember one day in particular. Suraj and I were discussing one of our wild schemes to go for a spin — something that was near impossible during curfew but seemed oh-so-tempting. We were deep into planning when the familiar click of a parallel line stopped us cold. Our hearts sank. Our fathers had been listening in on our talk all this while.

That spin? Yeah, it never happened. Our plan was foiled before it even got started. Such was the problem with those parallel lines — parents could eavesdrop without warning.

Sometimes, it wasn't just our fathers; girlfriends would call repeatedly, hoping to catch us when we were home alone, pretending it was a wrong number each time. "Oh, sorry, I think I dialed the wrong number,"they'd say, knowing full well they had dialed the right one. Our parents weren't fooled — they knew exactly who was calling and why. But there we were, blissfully unaware, living in a fool's paradise, thinking we were somehow outsmarting the adults.

Double trouble

Sam was the hero of his time, known for his charm and mischievous grin. He had not one, but two girlfriends: Esha and Nancy from the famous St. Peterson girls' school and, somehow, Sam had managed to juggle through the relationships without either girl finding out.

Until one fateful evening.

Esha had been trying to reach Sam all day. She'd been dialing his landline for hours, but the line was busy. Growing impatient, she picked up the phone and dialed '0' for the operator.

"Hello, operator?" she said sweetly, "Can you please help me connect with my friend Sam? His line has been busy all day, and this call is urgent."

The operator, a kind man who had heard countless stories of teenage love, agreed. "Hold on, Mam, let me check for you." A few clicks later, the operator whispered, "Your friend Sam's line is engaged. Should I interrupt?"

Esha smirked. "Yes, please."

The line connected, and to Esha's shock, she heard Nancy's voice at the other end.

"Sam, you're so sweet! When are we meeting next?" Nancy giggled.

Esha's eyes widened, but she kept quiet, listening in.

"Soon, babe. You know I miss you already."

Esha's blood boiled, but instead of hanging up, she decided to stay on, eavesdropping on the entire conversation. After a few minutes, Nancy sighed, "You've been talking to me for so long, Sam. Aren't you worried someone else might be calling?"

Sam, ever the confident smooth-talker, laughed. “Nah, I’ve got everything under control. No one’s going to interrupt us.” That was the cue Esha needed.

She cleared her throat loudly. “Oh really, Sam?”

The line fell silent. Sam froze.

“E-Esha? Is that you?” Sam stuttered.

“Yes, it’s me. And Nancy, are you still there?”

Nancy gasped on the other end. “What the — who is this?!”

“This is Esha. Sam’s other girlfriend.” Esha’s voice dripped with sarcasm. “I’ve been on the line this whole time, listening to your lovely conversation.”

Sam's voice cracked in desperation. “Esha, wait, I can explain —”

“Oh, I’m sure you can explain,” Esha snapped. “You’ve had plenty of practice, haven’t you?”

Nancy, now furious, jumped into the conversation. “Wait, what?! Sam, you’ve been two-timing me?!”

“It’s not what it looks like!” Sam pleaded.

“Oh, it is exactly what it looks like,” Esha replied coldly. “But don't worry, Nancy, we’ll both be dumping this guy together.”

Nancy paused, and then, surprisingly, she laughed. “You know what, Esha? That’s a great idea.”

Both girls started laughing, shattering Sam’s confidence into smithereens. He tried to salvage the situation, but the more he spoke, the worse it got.

“Sam, now consider yourself as single,” Esha said, before hanging up with a final, satisfied click.

Nancy, still on the line, sighed. “Goodbye, Sam. Enjoy your ‘hero’ days while they last.”

And with that, Sam sat there, staring at the receiver, wondering how he’d managed to go from having two girlfriends to none in a matter of minutes.

As for Esha and Nancy? They became good friends after that, often laughing about how they caught Sam red-handed thanks to a little help from the telephone operator.

And Sam? Well, he learned the hard way that you can't keep two girlfriends in the age of landlines and operators. Times were simple, so also technologies, but the thrill of rebellion felt just as real. The boredom of those days was never enough to dampen the spirits of our small, close-knit group. Especially when I had my big, square-sized stereophonic speakers blasting out music that filled up every corner of my room. Be it the Beatles, Air Supply, or Michael Jackson, they all seemed to be playing in my room all the time. I couldn't resist dancing to MJ's beats, aping his iconic moves, as if the energy in those songs could shake off my monotony.

Sam, on the other hand, was passionate about George Michael, or Kenny G's saxophone. And then there was Madonna, be it her voice, or her posters, Sam never had enough of it.

Suraj was yet another story. He was more into Hindi cinema. Kishore Kumar's voice was his lifeline. You'd catch him humming a Kishore number any given day.

I played the music so loud it would reach the farthest corners of our neighborhood. But no one ever complained. They wouldn't. After all they all gathered under our roof, not to complain about the noise, but to watch television — particularly Ramayan and Mahabharat, the epics that stopped India every time those were screened on Sunday mornings.

Those were not the days when people watched content such as Netflix or YouTube alone in the privacy of their rooms and on their mobile phones. Everything was on television and till a certain hour at night on Fridays – after which they screened an adult movie – everyone in the family could watch the idiot box, no censorship needed.

The moment the theme music of the Ramayan played on TV, a collective hush would descend across localities and in our TV room. Even the children sat still and wide-eyed with anticipation.

Neighbors, friends, uncles, aunts, and cousins would arrive in our living room to watch the epics. The elderly, with wrinkles on their faces and gleaming eyes, would sit in the best spots — closest to the television — while the younger ones squeezed in wherever they could, craning their necks for a better view. The stories weren't just entertaining they were lessons, passed down through the ages, retold with reverence. And each episode was an event in itself.

You could feel the room breathe as one, sighing in relief when a beloved character survived an approaching arrow, or gasping in sorrow when tragedy struck. The simplicity of it all was magical — the rich storytelling, the poetic dialogues, the meaningful lyrics, and the morals embedded in every line.

What I miss most is the shared experience. We didn't need streaming services with flashy trailers or constant notifications on our phones. The epic stories alone were enough to pull everyone together. They had the power to silence even the most talkative ones in the room, to hold the attention of young and old alike, and to spark conversations that carried on long after the credits rolled.

As the episodes would end, a different kind of chatter would fill the room. The elders would analyze the wisdom while the younger ones reenacted scenes, pretending to be warriors from the ancient texts. The air would be filled with laughter, but also with a deep sense of connection — a collective nostalgia for times long past and a reverence for stories that transcended time itself.

That was an era when television was a gathering place, a community in itself. Today, I look around and see everyone lost in their own screens, where shows seem to compete for shock value more than storytelling. Content today is available at the click of a button, but rarely does it hold the meaning those old serials carried. Back then, it wasn't just about watching; it was about experiencing something together. When we weren't busy with music, books and novels filled our spare time. Sam and Suraj were hooked on stories that felt like a world away from reality. They devoured Hardy Boys and Nancy Drew. There were also into "adult stuff" novels with complex plots, deeper themes.

I, on the other hand, preferred the color and excitement of comics. The Tintin series was a favorite, while The Archies provided an escape into the easy-going, carefree world of Riverdale. Then there were superheroes – Superman and Batman held me captive. And, I'd also flip through Filmfare to keep up with upcoming films and gossip.

Our tastes were different, but they shaped us in ways we probably didn't even realize back then. Each song, each book, each comic was more than a pastime — it was an escape, a momentary rebellion, a connection to something bigger than the humdrum of daily life.

The last days of curfew due to the Mandal Commission protests were filled with an electrifying buzz of excitement. It felt like the moment you unchain a bird from its cage — stretching its wings, ready to take to the skies. For us teenagers, the lockdown had been a strange, confining adventure. No stress, no financial worries, no adult responsibilities — just pure, unfiltered fun. Our main concern? Plotting our next mischief.

The DRDA gang — Sunny, Sandy, Sam, and Sagar — was no exception. We had watched enough action-packed Hollywood films to know that adventure was out there waiting for us, and we couldn't wait to claim it. "Jackie Chan's *Police Story*," "*Indiana Jones*," "*Superman*" — you name it. We had replayed these classics over and over again, making our own plans for when the lockdown would finally be lifted.

But being confined inside for so long was making Suraj antsy. He had, in a pre-lockdown moment of enthusiasm, rented a whole stack of VHS tapes — action thrillers, comedies and more.

He thought he'd breeze through them in a week, but now each passing day felt like a weight on his shoulders. "Ten bucks a day, man!" he moaned. "I'm going to lose a fortune!"

What Suraj didn't know was that the lockdown would stretch on far longer than any of us expected. As the days dragged by, those VHS tapes started to look more like expensive ornaments gathering dust. Every day the rental fee climbed by ten bucks, a debt building up faster than Suraj could calculate. He was trapped in a VHS nightmare.

And then, there was Jacky. Cool-headed, always thinking outside the box, Jacky wasn't about to let a few VHS rentals ruin anyone's day. "Boys, I've got a plan," he declared. Jacky always had the plan. "We'll pass the VHS tapes around, one by one, to each of us. Everyone watches it, and we split the rent. The vendor won't know who's holding the tapes, and by the time they get back, it'll be like they never left."

That was one heck of a plan. Pure teenage ingenuity. The moment lockdown ended, Suraj sprinted to the first meeting spot, tapes in hand like treasure. We passed them around like contraband, laughing as we dodged surcharges like seasoned outlaws. Each day, the vendor would scratch his head, wondering how one set of VHS tapes could be rented out for so long without burning a hole in anyone's pocket. It was like we were starring in our own heist film — except the loot was VHS tapes of cheesy action flicks.

The backdrop of all this fun and mischief was a country simmering in political tension. The Mandal Commission report had just ignited protests and unrest on the streets. College campuses were on fire — both metaphorically and literally — with debates on reservation, equality, and identity.

Even though we were just school kids, we couldn't escape the conversations. The streets were a mix of protestors, students on strike, and riot police enforcing curfews. But none of it could dampen our spirits or our wild sense of adventure.

Then came the day that still stands out in my mind like a half-finished VHS tape, paused at the perfect moment of chaos. Suraj had somehow gotten his hands on his father's Royal Enfield Bullet — a massive, growling beast of a bike that felt too large for even him. It was early morning, and the streets were quiet. The city was under curfew, thanks to the protests that had gotten out of hand the night before. But Suraj? He wasn't one to let a little thing like a citywide lockdown stop him from having an adventure.

"Hold on, boys!" Suraj shouted over the roaring engine, his voice full of excitement and a bit of madness. "This is going to be a ride you won't forget!"

Sam, always the cautious one, clutched the backseat for dear life. "Slow down, man! You're going to get us killed!" But there was a spark of thrill in his eyes that he couldn't hide.

I, on the other hand, was too busy grinning from ear to ear, the wind whipping through my hair, the thrill of speed pumping through my veins. Suraj's laughter echoed in my ears, a sound that would forever remind me of our reckless, joyous youth.

The roads were empty, the world still waking up as we sped towards the riverside. It was our favorite spot — away from school, away from the prying eyes of teachers and parents, where we could just be ourselves.

"Get on, boys," Suraj said, with that grin of his face that always meant trouble. Sam, ever the cautious one, was muttering something about how this was a terrible idea, but he couldn't resist the thrill that came with riding a bike down an empty road.

We sped through the narrow lanes of our town, the bike roaring as it carried the three of us like some kind of three headed beast. The smell of the river, mixed with the damp earth and the morning mist, filled the air as we approached our favorite haunt — a lonely stretch of the riverbank where we'd spent countless afternoons chucking stones and dreaming big.

As we turned a corner, Suraj suddenly slammed on the brakes, the bike screeching to a halt. The tires kicked up dust, and for a moment I thought we were going to crash. But it wasn't the bike that scared us — it was what was lying across the road.

A crocodile. A real, massive, terrifying crocodile, just lounging in the middle of the road like it owned the place.

"Holy crap," I muttered, my voice barely above a whisper. Suraj, usually fearless, was uncharacteristically silent, his eyes wide with a mix of awe and confusion.

"What now?" Sam asked, his voice shaking as he clung to the back of the bike.

But Suraj, being Suraj, did the unthinkable. He got off the bike and started walking towards the beast. "We're not leaving without a closer look."

The three of us stood there, inching closer to the creature, as if drawn by some unseen force. The crocodile's eyes followed us, and for a second, I was certain we were going to end up as its breakfast. But it didn't move. It just lay there, watching us like we were the most boring thing it had seen all day. Eventually, as the sun climbed higher in the sky, the crocodile lazily blinked and began to move. We all took a step back, hearts pounding, but it merely turned and slowly ambled towards the river, disappearing into the water with a soft splash.

"Well," Suraj said, breaking the silence once more. "That was something."

“Yeah,” Sam agreed, his voice shaky but filled with the kind of excitement that only comes from narrowly avoiding a brush with danger. “Let’s not do that again.”

Just as we started to breathe again, a distant siren broke the silence. The police. We’d forgotten about the curfew. Our hearts started racing for a whole new reason.

“Run!” Suraj shouted, jumping back onto the bike. Sam and I didn’t need to be told twice. We sped off, the sound of the siren growing louder behind us, the wind once again whipping through our hair as we tore down the empty road. For a moment, it felt like we’d escaped everything — the curfew, the protests, everything except the thrill of being alive.

But the cops weren’t far behind. As we reached the main road, we saw them — a barricade had been set up, and a group of officers were waiting for us. There was no way out.

We were caught.

“Looks like the adventure’s over,” Suraj muttered as we slowed to a stop, his grin never fading even as the police dragged us to the station. They let us off with a warning, but we knew we’d be in for it once our parents found out.

Years later, whenever I think back to that day, I always have a smile. Suraj was the daredevil of our group, the one who lived life full throttle and never backed down from anything. He was the one who could make us laugh in the face of danger, who turned even the most mundane of trips into an unforgettable adventure.

But he will miss the reunion, not because he didn’t want to come, but because life had other plans. A fatal accident took him away from us too soon, leaving behind memories that are as vivid as they are painful. We lost our first friend. Losing our first friend feels like losing a piece of our soul — the one who shared meals, laughter, and joy with us was no more, leaving our bike seat empty forever. The deepest pain lies in not being there to say goodbye.

Every time I think of him, I can still hear the roar of his Bullet, the laughter that followed every daring stunt, and the way he'd say, "Don't worry, boys, we're just getting started."

Those were the days — days of carefree joy, of dangerous pranks, of being young and feeling invincible. And even though those days are long gone, they live in my heart, a reminder of a true friend who showed us all how to truly live.

Reunion: Opening Scene

Location – Centurion school Time 9: 30 AM

The sun shone bright as I approached the rusty old gate of my school, the same I'd dashed through countless times as a kid. The air was thick with nostalgia. I stood there for a moment, my hand hovering over the gate's cold iron bar, trying to reconcile the years that had passed. The building looked the same, yet somehow different — worn by time, like an old friend I haven't seen in decades. I also saw something else at the gate, a fizzy soda bottle which used to be my favorite drink. I recalled how I used to pick the bottle and gently press the marble with my thumb, enjoying the pop sound it made before the aroma of soda hit you. Before I entered the gate, I remembered also that this was the same school that had denied me admission initially.

A Father's Dream, A Principal's Change of Heart

It was a sunny morning when my father took me by the hand and led me into the school. I was too young to understand the gravity of what was about to happen, but I knew this day was important. My father's grip was firm yet gentle, his calloused hands telling the story of a man who had worked hard all his life — just not in the way that the world measured success.

We stood before the grand entrance of the school, a place that held the promise of a different future. For me, this was the doorway to knowledge, to opportunity, to dreams my father could never have dreamed for himself. But for him, it was a battleground — one where he would have to fight for something that many took for granted.

The principal, Mr. James, a stern man with a sharp gaze that seemed to pierce through anyone who dared stand before him, sat in his chair. My father introduced himself, explaining that he wanted me to attend the school. I stood quietly beside him, clutching his hand.

But the principal, without even glancing at me, shook his head. “I’m sorry,” he said in a tone as cold as the polished floors of his office. “We have certain standards. Your son doesn’t meet the criteria for admission.”

My father, puzzled, asked, “What criteria? He’s just a child. He hasn’t even had the chance to prove himself yet.”

The principal looked my father up and down, and with a faint, dismissive smile, said, “You are not educated. How do you expect your son to succeed if you can’t guide him? If the father isn’t educated, the child will likely follow the same path.”

The words stung. I saw pain lines make a fold on my father’s forehead, but he stood tall, unwilling to let the moment pass without defending the future he dreamed of for me. For a moment, I feared he might give up and turn away, but he didn’t. He looked straight into the principal’s eyes and said something that still echoes in my heart.

“Sir,” he began, his voice steady and filled with quiet resolve, “just because I’m not educated, does that mean my son should be uneducated too? Is it his destiny to be held back by my limitations?”

The principal leaned back in his chair, clearly surprised by the response. My father continued, his voice growing stronger, “I may not know how to read or write, but I know the value of education. I know what it means to want a better life for my child, to want him to achieve things I never could. Isn’t that what all parents want? If I can’t teach him, that’s why I brought him here — to you, to this school, so he can learn from people who know better.”

The room fell silent. I glanced at the principal, hoping to see a change in his expression. His eyes softened, and for the first time, he truly looked at me, as if seeing more than just a boy standing with his father. He saw potential, a future that was not yet written.

My father's words hung in the air, simple yet profound. The principal sat quietly for what felt like an eternity before speaking again, his voice no longer cold but thoughtful. "You are right," he said slowly. "A child's future should not be limited by the circumstances of his parents. Your son will be given admission… as an exception."

I didn't fully understand what had just happened, but I could feel the weight of it. My father had won something far greater than just a seat in the classroom for me. He had opened a door to a world that might otherwise have been closed. And as we walked out of that office, I looked up at him and saw the pride in his eyes — a pride that wasn't just for me but for himself, for standing his ground.

That day, I realized that education is not just about books and lessons; it's about the belief that everyone, no matter where they come from or who their parents are, deserves a chance to learn and grow. My father may not have been able to teach me algebra or history, but he taught me something far more valuable — that courage and determination can change even the most unyielding hearts.

And so, with every lesson I learned in that school, I carried with me the knowledge that my father's dreams were planted in me, and that I wasn't just living for myself — I was living for the man who believed in me when the world did not.

Back to the reunion day at school

As my fingers gripped the gate and pulled it open with a creek, a wave of sensations hit me. The soft, distant echo of the school bell rang in my ears, a sound that made my heart skip a beat. It wasn't just any bell — it was *the* bell, the one that signaled both freedom and detention, the same one that warned of exams and promised recess.

Suddenly, footsteps. Not real ones, but the unmistakable cadence of the school parade. The rhythmic thud of boots hitting the ground in unison, echoing through the empty courtyard. I could almost see them — the students, my younger self, marching with precision, my shoes tapping out a beat that still lived in the cracks of these pavements.

Then, out of nowhere, voices — voices calling my name, sharp and clear. Not just any voice — my friends from back in the day. "Hey, hurry up! You're late!" The shout came from across the field, and for a split second, I turned my head, half expecting to see them standing there, waving frantically, backpacks slung over their shoulders. I could even feel the wind from the soccer ball that narrowly missed my head in their usual chaotic, friendly fire.

My heart pounded. It was overwhelming — electrifying, as if the school itself was alive, buzzing with memories that refused to die. Every brick seemed to hum with energy, every leaf rustling in the wind whispered stories of the past. I was lost in it, standing in the twilight between what was and what is, haunted by echoes that refused to fade.

As I stepped into the familiar reunion hall, the bright lights softened against the buzz of laughter and conversation. My heart raced as I looked down at the special T-shirt we ordered for the reunion, its soft fabric clinging to me like a second skin, adorned with memories that felt both distant and immediate. Each step I took felt heavier with anticipation, the same way I'd felt on the first day of school, not knowing who I'd meet, what mischief we'd get into, or how the day would unfold.

And then, there they were — my friends. Some older, wiser, a few with laugh lines that hadn't been there before, but beneath the surface, the same energy, the same mischief gleamed in their eyes. I approached them, unable to contain my grin. It was as if the years between us had dissolved into nothingness. The hugs were tight, full of unsaid words, the kind that only lifelong friends could understand.

The reunion committee announced the first activity — Attendance. A sharp wave of nostalgia hit me. I closed my eyes, transported back to the classroom. The roll call... it used to be the gateway to freedom. I could almost hear the teacher's voice, monotonous, reading out names. "Present," we'd say, eager to get it over with, knowing what came next. The thrill of sneaking out right after. The way we'd slip past the gates, heartbeats quickening, bags slung over our shoulders, walking briskly towards the world outside — the city, the movies, the ice creams, the adventures that awaited us.

It was a scene straight out of a military march, yet with a dash of suspense that could rival any Hollywood blockbuster. The school bell rang, echoing like the sound of an impending battle. As if on cue, every single student froze — backs straight, eyes gleaming with determination.

The roll call was over. Now came the moment we had all been waiting for — the march to the stage. We stood shoulder to shoulder, hands tightly clasped, the grip of solidarity so intense that it felt like we were bound by a sacred, unspoken pact. The air was electric, thick with the weight of impending glory.

With military precision, we began our journey. Each step reverberated through the courtyard, like the heartbeat of an unstoppable force. The teachers watched in awe, unsure whether they were witnessing the rise of a disciplined student army or the start of something far grander — a revolution, perhaps?

Our eyes remained fixed on the stage ahead, our movements in perfect sync, as if choreographed by fate itself. Nothing could break our concentration — not the rustling of the leaves, not even the distant sound of birds, which might as well have been trumpeting our arrival.

And then, as we neared the stage, the wind picked up. It was as if the universe was acknowledging our power, showering us with gusts of triumph. We were no longer just students. We were legends in the making, marching to take our rightful place in history.

Title: The Reunion Drama

Location: Centurion Hall

A grand hall decked in school colors, the stage set with a mic, a podium, and a banner that read "Reunion and Felicitation Ceremony". The teachers, now retired or at the peak of their careers, sat in the front row, awaiting the honors from their once-young pupils. Students of our batch were all dressed smartly, reminiscing their school days while waiting for the event to begin.

"Ah, the grandeur of the school reunion – where memories are revived, teachers are showered with gratitude, and of course, long-forgotten rivalries make a surprise comeback! And leading this ceremonious event was Dhruv, the head of the NCC group – known for his discipline, punctuality, and, the kind of guy who probably still wakes up at 5 a.m. for a jog." Watching Dhruv again I was transported back in time.

The NCC Chronicles: A Wild Chase

Don't know how it feels to be at Centurion on a Saturday morning these days. But in the good old days in the '90s, the school's corridors would reverberate with laughter, chatter and footsteps. Because some of us would gather, this time in a different uniform, and kick up a lot of dust. This time we weren't there just as students of the school, but also as NCC cadets, dressed in crisp khaki, caps perched neatly on our heads. Dhruv, our troop commander, commanded respect not only because of his skills but because of his humility and charisma.

Our team was an eclectic mix of characters: Deepak, Ramesh, Sashi, Akash, Pandya -- famously known as Pablo, and I. I can safely say we were the heart and soul of the squad. Deepak was known for his silent dedication, Ramesh was the joker in the pack, while Pablo had a knack for getting into trouble. Sashi was the calm, composed troubleshooter, and Akash the daredevil, always ready to take up any challenge.

Our NCC instructor, Mr. Rao, was a force of nature. With his steel-gray mustache and razor-sharp glare, he ran the NCC squad like a drill sergeant. There was no room for tardiness, no place for excuses. If you were late, you paid for it — usually by doing a few laps around the field. Mr. Rao knew how to discipline the most rebellious of boys.

Saturdays had a rhythm of their own. The sessions started with rigorous drills, shooting practice, obstacle courses, a run on the grounds and then the real thing most of us actually signed up for – the samosas and jalebis and endless rounds of banter. It was a closely knit group, but with seniors and juniors thrown in together, there were always spirited debates, some leg-pulling and some hilarious moments that lingered in our minds long after we had returned home.

I remember I would be trying to finish some homework in the lazy afternoon when I would be startled out of an approaching reverie with the thought of Dhruv suddenly calling out "*Saavdhaan* (Attention)". And then I would smile, imagining he was putting all of us at ease with "*Bishram* (Rest)".

One particular Saturday is still etched on my mind. It was not very different from other Saturdays when it began. The sun was just rising as Dhruv and our team assembled on the field, ready to march. Everyone except Pablo, that is. He came sprinting, he had reached late. His excuse? He had overslept, again. Mr. Rao's gaze turned icy. He instantly pointed to the edge of the field. "Run. Ten laps," he ordered. Pablo, groaning inwardly, started doing the laps. The rest of us were thanking our stars we had not overslept that day. But just as Pablo began his third lap, a stray dog, a wild-looking, scruffy mutt with mismatched fur, wandered into the field. At first, it seemed harmless, sniffing around as Pablo jogged past. Then, it suddenly leaped forward, barking furiously.

Pablo, startled, took off at full speed, and the dog—now fully invested in the chase—followed. What started as a routine punishment had quickly turned into a mad sprint, with Pablo running for dear life, the dog closing in behind.

The sight was so hilarious Sashi was rolling on the ground, clutching his stomach, while Deepak tried to egg Pablo on, only ending up strengthening the dog's resolve further.

Even Dhruv, who was usually very composed, at first smiled, then began giggling before he couldn't hold back any more. Pablo, arms flailing, was running like never before, the dog closing in, nipping at his heels.

"Faster, Pablo!" yelled Akash. "Show that dog who's the boss!"

Even Mr. Rao was having trouble maintaining his stern demeanor. We caught him grinning briefly before he quickly turned away to hide his expression.

Finally, after what seemed like eternity, Pablo managed to dash to the refreshments table and hop on, as the dog skidded to a stop, barking at him from below.

Mr. Rao, still maintaining a sliver of authority, walked over to Pablo, shaking his head. With a faint smile playing on his lips, he said, "Pablo, next time you're late, I'll make sure the dog's waiting for you at the start of the lap."

Everyone laughed, and Pablo, still catching his breath, managed a sheepish grin. "Maybe, I should carry some biscuits for the dog next time," he panted.

So NCC was not just about drills and parades; or of wishing that the commander would call out "*dahine dekh* (look right)" when a girl who was everyone's heartthrob was passing by, maybe cycling to a teacher's house on the school premises for a tuition; or about hitting bull's-eye at shooting camp to make even a dour Mr. Rao yell "brilliant". It was a mix of various memories on top of which was that of Pablo doing umpteen laps to stay ahead of a growling dog.

Back to the present

Taking a steady breath, Dhruv leaned into the microphone, his voice clear but reverent.

"Good morning, everyone," he began, his words laced with a quiet gravity. "Today is not just any day. It's a day of remembrance, of reflection..." He paused for a moment, as if letting the weight of those words sink into the hearts of those seated before him. "...and most importantly, a day of showing respect. Respect for the teachers who shaped us, who molded us into the people we've become."

There was a brief silence, the kind that happens when the truth of the moment is too profound for immediate applause. Dhruv stood tall, waiting for the emotion in the room to settle before continuing, aware that his words were a bridge to the past, binding us all together in a shared legacy.

The crowd, though admiring Dhruv's speech, were a little tense, because they knew what was coming next. The speeches. The avalanche of speeches.

Dhruv smiled warmly as he glanced across the room, the weight of nostalgia evident in his voice. "I want to especially thank all the teachers who made time to be with us today," he said, pausing to let his gaze linger on the familiar faces that had shaped their lives so many years ago. "Your presence means more than words can express."

The room, filled with a blend of quiet murmurs and soft smiles, seemed to hang on his every word.

Taking a deep breath, Dhruv continued, his voice steady but laced with emotion. "Now, I would like to invite Arshad, our esteemed Head Boy, to say a few words."

He gestured toward the podium, stepping back to give space as Arshad rose to speak, the soft clatter of chairs the only sound as anticipation rippled through the crowd

Enter Arshad, looking charming and nostalgic.

Arshad's smile stretched from ear to ear as he looked around the familiar faces gathered in the old school hall. He stepped forward, his voice warm and full of nostalgia.

"Hello, everyone!" he exclaimed, his tone light yet full of excitement. "What a fantastic moment to be back here with all of you. I don't know about you, but just stepping into this building brought back a flood of memories."

The room buzzed with quiet chuckles and nods of agreement. Arshad's eyes gleamed with mischief as he added, "Especially sneaking into the staff room for a 'borrowed' piece of chalk."

Laughter rippled through the crowd, their shared past lighting up their faces as they were drawn back to those mischievous school days.

The crowd laughed, nodding in agreement, clearly already hooked on by Arshad's charm.

Arshad stood at the podium, the soft murmur of the crowd fading into an expectant silence. His fingers lightly gripped the edges of the wooden stand, a nervous smile playing on his lips. The reunion hall was packed with familiar faces, some etched with the lines of time, others still carrying the youthful glow he remembered. But today, his attention was focused on a different group, seated in the front row — his teachers.

Taking a deep breath, he began, his voice warm and steady. "I know we've all had a lot of fun reminiscing tonight," Arshad said, glancing around with a knowing grin, "but jokes aside, we're here today to honor our beloved teachers."

A ripple of applause followed, and he paused for a moment, his gaze softening as he looked at the teachers who had shaped his youth.

"For me," he continued, "each of you left a lasting impression. I don't think I truly understood the impact of your lessons back then, but now, after all these years, I realize just how deeply they've shaped who I am."

He smiled, a hint of nostalgia tugging at the corners of his mouth. "If I ever succeed in life," Arshad said, his voice filled with sincerity, "it's because of the lessons you taught — both in and outside the classroom. You didn't just teach us subjects; you taught us how to think, how to question, and how to be better people."

There was a brief pause, the room holding its collective breath. His eyes scanned the faces of his former teachers, each one filled with pride, humility, and a touch of amusement.

"Thank you," he said, his voice firm with emotion, "for putting up with our pranks, for being patient with our mistakes, and for giving us knowledge that still guides us today."

The hall erupted into applause, a heartfelt acknowledgment of the gratitude that filled the room. Arshad stepped back, feeling the warmth of the moment wash over him, knowing that no matter how much time had passed, the bond between student and teacher remained unchanged, a testament to the power of those early lessons that had stood the test of time.

Dhruv stepped back to the microphone, his smile still lingering though his posture remained as stiff as before. "Thank you, Arshad, for those wonderful words," he said, his voice carrying a note of formality despite the warmth of the occasion.

A brief pause followed as he glanced over the audience, then continued, "Now, I would like to invite some of our respected teachers to say a few words."

The crowd shifted slightly, anticipating the next speaker.

"We begin with Mrs. Sharma," he announced, the familiar name drawing a few smiles. Mrs. Sharma, the favorite Mathematics teacher, was known to many not just for her lessons, but for the patient guidance she had given over the years.

Mrs. Sharma took the stage, her gentle smile radiating warmth as she addressed us. "My dear students," she began, her voice laced with nostalgia, "I remember each of you as if it were just yesterday. This school, and the memories we've shared together, will forever hold a cherished place in my heart. Thank you for this honor."

Her words faltered as tears welled in her eyes, and a profound silence enveloped the room. We all rose to our feet in reverence, acknowledging the depth of her emotions. As the quite stretched, I closed my eyes, and a distant memory from years past surfaced in my mind, vivid and unbidden.

The Great Tuition Fees scam

It was a time when students from different schools would come to Mrs. Sharma for Math's tuitions. Her students spoke of her brilliance and parents clamored to enroll their children under her tutelage. Among those who joined her classes were also people from our mischievous group — Sam, Sachin, Jonty and I. We were known for our pranks, charm, and uncanny ability to spin even the dullest situations into a whirlwind of excitement.

However, what no one could have predicted — was the grand scheme that was about to unfold. We, with pockets empty but dreams of living large, devised a plan that would go down in the history of student shenanigans.

The plan was simple, or so it seemed.

Each of us collected monthly tuition fees from our unsuspecting parents, pretending to be eager disciples of Mrs. Sharma. "Mathematics is essential for our future!" we told our parents. "Mrs. Sharma is the best! We will ace every test under her guidance!" Our parents, impressed by our sudden thirst for knowledge, showered us with funds every month with high expectations.

But we boys never intended to attend the sessions. Oh no. The minute we stepped out of home for Mrs. Sharma's tuition class, we would change our minds and head towards our whims and fancies.

From there, we would embark on legendary adventures with our newly acquired 'pocket money.' While our classmates puzzled over algebra, Sam and I were racing down to the arcade. Sachin and Jonty were at the ice-cream parlor, treating themselves to towering sundaes that could rival any skyscraper. Sam, always spent his cut on an outrageous collection of comic books and flashy gadgets. Our lives had become a paradise of forbidden indulgence, a hidden mystery beneath our parents' proud eyes. This went on for months.

But in every tale of mischief, there is always one outlier.

In our tale the outlier was Prashant. He had been a part of our group, privy to our clandestine meetings and wild ideas. Yet, when the plan was pitched, he wrinkled his nose and said, "I think I'll stick to the classes, boys." The others scoffed, but he stuck to his guns. He attended every tuition class religiously, becoming a favorite of Mrs. Sharma.

It wasn't long before Mrs. Sharma began to notice something odd. Prashant was always there, but the others, us? Our seats were suspiciously empty. Suspicion grew, and soon Mrs. Sharma, with her sharp intuition, hatched a plan of her own. She waited patiently, letting us believe that we were invincible, until the day of the grand class test arrived.

Sam, Sachin, Jonty & I swaggered into the room that day, confident that we could clear the test with a few clever guesses and a lot of luck. We hadn't opened a single book, let alone attended enough classes to know what the test was even about. As we looked at the paper, our faces went pale. It was an impossible web of math problems that looked like pictograms. We all failed the test.

But the real twist came after the test. Mrs. Sharma summoned us one by one, her piercing gaze on the test papers cutting through our bravado.

"You thought I wouldn't know?" she said, her voice calm but with an edge that could slice through steel. "Pocket money over mathematics? Sneaking out while your friend Prashant put in the hard work?" Our secret was out.

Prashant, on the other hand, became her star pupil, a living testament to the power of discipline. The group? We were grounded for weeks, our parents furious about the wasted tuition fees. We had enjoyed our secret fortune for a time, but in the end, the price of our antics was steep.

As for Prashant, he went on to ace every math test, winning accolades, while we learned a valuable lesson: the real treasure wasn't the pocket money but what we could've gained in Mrs. Sharma's class... though the ice-cream sundaes were pretty hard to beat.

Miss Sharma's speech was short, sweet, and warmly received. Hoping she forgave us for our act.

Next came Mr. Patel, who shared a humorous story about his time teaching – the crowd lapped it up.

Dhruv cleared his throat, his gaze sweeping over the gathered crowd. "Thank you, Mr. Patel," he said, his voice steady and appreciative. "And now… Mr. Andrew, please come up and share your thoughts."

The room collectively shifted. They knew what was coming. Mr. Andrew, our English teacher, famous for his long-winded lectures, walked up to the stage.

Mr. Andrew's voice echoed with the weight of nostalgia as he addressed the room. "Thank you, Dhruv. Before we dive into the evening's festivities, I'd like to take us all on a brief journey down memory lane. Picture this: it's the year your batch was in Grade 10…"

The crowd listens politely at first. But then Mr. Andrew's speech goes on and on. He goes into detail about the curriculum, the teaching methods, and the shortage of chalks ... his own future plans.

From the audience, a hushed whisper cut through the ambient murmur. “Did we just get transported back to English class? Someone pinch me please!” A second voice chimed in, equally bemused, “I thought we’d escaped this once we graduated!”

As Mr. Andrew drones on, the teachers start to look uncomfortable, and some students begin to subtly check their watches. The atmosphere grows heavy with a sense of déjà vu.

It was starting to feel like an interminable sermon. Could someone please put an end to this relentless monologue?

“Can somebody take his wicket please,” said Deepak, the captain of our cricket team looking at me in a very resigned manner.

I then gestured to Dhruv to put an end to Mr. Andrew’s unending lecture.

Finally, after what felt like ages, Dhruv, ever the disciplined leader, stepped in, clearing his throat.

Seizing the moment, Dhruv interjected with a courteous nod. "Mr. Andrew, Sir, your speech was truly enlightening. However, I must apologize for the interruption. We have a cricket match slated to start soon. As you know, we have a particular fondness for keeping to our schedules."

The crowd breathed a collective sigh of relief. Mr. Andrew stopped, looked mildly surprised, but nodded graciously.

"Ah, yes, of course. Cricket. Always important! I’ll wrap it up." Mr. Andrew said.

The crowd erupted in applause as Dhruv took charge again, giving the students and teachers the breather they were all silently hoping for.

And so, with Mr. Andrew’s speech over, the crowd moved on to refreshments, where everyone mingled, laughed, chatted, and thanked our lucky stars that Dhruv saved the day."

Refreshments for teachers arrived and arrangements began for the group photo session with everyone eagerly squeezing in. The teachers beamed proudly, while the students, now adults, huddled around them, capturing the moment that will forever stand as a reminder of the bond they shared.

Just then Jonty the champ and the darling of our batch with his wit and perfect comic timing began confronting Mr. Chaturvedi our famous Art Teacher, popularly known as the White Man of our school, who was looking for his favorite south Indian dish "Dosa" at the refreshment table. The very word "Dosa" again drifted me back to a time when a humorous incident had taken place.

Jonty was a legendary figure in our batch — the kind of guy who could turn the most ordinary day into a rollercoaster of chaos. Mischief practically oozed from his pores, and he was always up to something that would leave us in stitches.

Location: Sun Restaurant during School lunch break

One afternoon we all decided to head to the local restaurant, a small joint famous for its South Indian dishes. Just as we were settling in, our arts teacher, Mr. Chaturvedi, who was famous for his blindingly white uniform, walked in. Seriously, this guy had a wardrobe that was whiter than a toothpaste commercial, and he wore it every single day. Even the scooter he rode was white in color. It seemed he had a fascination for the color "white", which was unique and exceptional. He wore white shoes, even the socks were white in color and we wondered what on earth he wore or sported that wasn't white in color.

Jonty, with that devilish grin of his, nudged us as Mr. Chaturvedi took a seat nearby and ordered his favorite dish — dosa. Before we could blink, Jonty had summoned the waiter with a dramatic wave and asked, in his most innocent tone, "Do you have a white dosa? Our guest here only eats things that match his outfit."

The entire table erupted in laughter. We were clutching our stomachs, trying not to fall off our chairs. Mr. Chaturvedi, however, wasn't amused. His face turned red like the ketchup bottle on the table, and he shot Jonty a glare that could have fried an egg. "Jonty!" he bellowed, his voice echoing through the restaurant, "You think you're funny, don't you?"

But Jonty, unfazed as always, just leaned back in his chair, flashing that same grin, as if to say, "Of course, I'm hilarious." It wasn't as hilarious the next day when Mr. Chaturvedi unleashed his anger through the wooden duster; Jonty was wincing in pain, his palms closed, by the time Mr. Chaturvedi was done with the duster treatment and was leaving the classroom.

Jonty's mischief wasn't limited to that. He was just getting started. He was a genius when it came to English, especially vocabulary, and he knew how to work it to his advantage. During the morning assembly news, when it was his turn to read the news, he had the whole school holding their breath — not because of his impeccable pronunciation, but because of his choice of headlines. Jonty had a knack for picking out the weirdest news stories, the kind that made you raise an eyebrow and wonder where on Earth he found them. In one of his news flashes in the early morning assembly he articulated his thoughts in his own unique way. "In a dramatic turn of events, politicians continue their heated debates over the budget, while business tycoons play their own game of chess in boardrooms, strategizing for the next quarter's profits. Meanwhile, the cricket field is no less intense, with India winning another thrilling match, sending fans into a frenzy. In a surprising twist, a group of cheerleaders – "the sexy girl's squad" — stole the spotlight for a few moments with their dance moves, leaving even the politicians and businessmen momentarily distracted! Now, who's winning again? Seems like everyone's got their eyes on the wrong field!"

And he made sure to emphasize on words like "sexy girls", triggering a wave of awkward coughs and shuffling of feet among the teachers and students alike. The "sexy girls" mentioned was purely intended for comic effect.

But that fateful day, he pushed it too far. The principal, who usually sat through the assemblies with a stoic expression, suddenly snapped his head up. "Jonty!" he boomed, his voice cutting through the giggles that were already starting to ripple through the hall. Jonty was promptly yanked off the stage and spent the rest of the day explaining his "editorial choices" in the principal's office.

Yet, despite all the trouble he got into, Jonty was the life of our batch. He had this infectious energy that made even the most boring moments hilarious. Whether it was turning a simple joke into a full-blown skit or just making a sly comment that had us in splits, Jonty never missed a chance to bring a little chaos and fun into our lives. And honestly, we wouldn't have had it any other way.

Dhruv (as the group got ready for the photo): "Let's make this an unforgettable memory!"

"And thus, the reunion with the teachers' session ended in peace, laughter & nostalgia, Except for Mr. Andrew – he was seen later trying to finish his speech on the cricket field." The much-awaited Reunion cricket match was yet to begin and everyone marched towards the playground for some live action.

The Reunion Cricket Match: A Trip Down Memory Lane

Location – The school playground

The sun was setting over the old school ground, casting long shadows across the freshly painted white lines of the cricket pitch. Deepak stood at the edge, gripping a cricket bat, as the rest of our schoolmates gathered around, warming up for their long-awaited reunion match. It had been years since we last saw each other, but the connection we shared — through cricket — was eternal. The team was divided into two by our most talented player Deepak who chose to don the hat of umpire.

As I watched my friends joke around and get in position, my mind wandered back to that special match, the one that defined our school years.

It was decades ago. Deepak and our group of close friends were juniors, filled with the zeal of youth and a burning passion for cricket. We weren't just playing cricket; we lived, breathed, and worshipped it. Every lunch break was spent on the field, dreaming of one day defeating our seniors in school — the undisputed champions of the annual cricket tournament.

The day of the tournament was a crisp morning. The juniors, led by Deepak, were dismissed by most as mere challengers, no match for the seniors' experience. But Deepak had a plan. He had been observing how the seniors played for weeks, and with each ball bowled during practice, he had grown more confident.

In the meeting, the air was thick with tension. Our friends, though excited, looked nervous. "We're really going up against the seniors, Deepak? They've got Ryan — the school's best fast bowler. He broke a stump with his last delivery," I said nervously.

Deepak smiled with a glint of mischief in his eye. "That's exactly what we are going to focus on. Everyone fears them. But not us."

The match began. The seniors won the toss and chose to bat first. The opening overs were brutal. The seniors' top batsmen smashed the ball all over the field, amassing runs with ease. Their captain, Ryan, looked like he had already sealed the game, flashing his signature smirk from the pavilion. The air was thick with tension. I remember walking up to the umpire before my first over, trying to look all serious, and said, "Excuse me, sir, I'm a right-arm fast bowler." The umpire nearly choked on his whistle laughing. "Right arm what? Fast? We'll see about that, kid!" he chuckled. My heart sank a little, but Deepak patted me on the back, "Don't worry about him. Just bowl like your life depends on it! I did my best. It was a decent over with no wickets down.

But then came Deepak's moment, as he took fast wickets and then took a clever decision by passing the ball to Abhay, our secret weapon, who had recently mastered the art of swing bowling. With a perfectly timed delivery, Abhay sent the senior captain's off-stump flying, and the game took a dramatic turn. Thereafter wickets fell like nine pins, in the form of catches taken by our famous wicketkeeper Imran who left no stone unturned to get them in his gloves. Catches win matches. The seniors, once so confident, now looked shaky. The crowd, previously indifferent, was on its feet, roaring with excitement as the juniors took control. The seniors were stunned. They managed to scrape together 90 runs, but I could see the disbelief on their faces as they trudged off the field. We had done the impossible — we had humbled the mighty seniors to some extent.

Then it was our turn to bat. Every run felt like a victory, every boundary a statement. Our openers started slowly and gave us the hope for victory. They were glued to the pitch and gave us the start we desired. The scores were promising and we didn't give up. When Deepak strode out to bat, the entire school ground was cheering him. Facing Ryan, the fastest bowler in the district, I remembered every practice, every hour spent perfecting his cover drive. With each ball, the tension mounted. Deepak played a big innings by hammering every bowl to the boundary. We were almost close to a mighty dream win.

But soon, the seniors' bowlers found their rhythm back, and wickets started tumbling. Deepak, our cricketing Hercules, was the last man standing. He turned to me and said, "Just hang in there, don't do anything stupid." But of course, I did something stupid. Their bowler delivered a ball that could've been mistaken for a rocket, and I, in all my glory, swung wildly — and missed. The ball clattered into the stumps, and that was that.

We lost by just a few runs, but the school was talking about our heroic performance. We were the underdog champions in everyone's eyes, and suddenly, we were famous! Kids we didn't even know started asking for autographs — on their notebooks, on their hands, even on a few cricket bats! It was as if we had won the World Cup.

Our passion for cricket only grew after that. We joined the local cricket club under Deepak's wing, dreaming of one day playing professionally. But then, we met Mr. Ghosh — the club's coach, who had the charm of a grumpy bear and a vocabulary that would make a sailor blush. "Are you lost, boy, searching for the balls your father never had?" he barked at me after a particularly poor catch drop. That was the last straw.

One by one, our group started dropping out. Cricket, the game we once loved, had become a battlefield of insults and humiliation. Our dreams of glory faded, and we returned to playing with paper balls and makeshift bats during lunch breaks.

But Deepak, our unstoppable captain, kept going. He broke through the barriers and went on to play in big tournaments, living out the dream we had all shared. As for the rest of us, cricket became a fond memory — a game we'd reminisce about over tiffin boxes and during nostalgic lunchtime chats.

In the end, the game didn't beat us; life did. But those matches, those moments on the pitch, they're etched in our hearts forever — because, for a brief, shining moment, we were cricket legends.

Back at the reunion, I snapped out of my daydream as the umpire called for the last ball to be bowled. My heart still raced when I thought about that match — a defining moment of our youth. Now, as me and old friends prepared to relive our glory days, the same excitement bubbled up inside me.

Location: Classroom

I stood at the edge of the cricket field, watching the group of my old classmates as they made their way towards the school building. The reunion cricket match had ended, but the conversations and laughter hadn't. A few of the guys were now heading to our old classrooms for a trip down memory lane.

As we all walked, I hesitated for a moment. A tug of nostalgia pulled at me. We passed an old classroom, untouched by time. The chipped paint on the walls, the faded posters, the worn-out desks — everything brought back waves of memories.

As the others laughed and exchanged stories, I found myself drifting into my own thoughts. I gazed and wandered to the desk by the window. It was her desk, Sana my school-time obsession.

I walked slowly towards it, tracing my fingers along the edges, the air thick with memories. It had been so long, but in that moment, it felt like yesterday.

At the reunion, the memories were unfolding beautifully. Laughter echoed through the hall as old friends reconnected, shared stories, and reminisced about the good old days. I was sitting with a small group, exchanging light banter, when my friend, Ravi, leaned in with a grin.

"So, come on then," Ravi said, eyes twinkling. "Everyone's been sharing their tales of teenage crushes and love stories. You've been quiet. Got any romantic tale or scene to share with us?"

I chuckled, taking a sip of my soft drink, stalling for a moment. The memories came flooding back, and for a split second, my mind drifted to a different time — a simpler time when a certain girl used to make my heart race.

"Well, I don't know if it's all that romantic," I began, a playful smile tugging at my lips, "but there was this one moment that has stayed with me."

The group leaned in, curious now.

"It was the last day of school," I continued, "and I remember walking out to the schoolyard, and there she was.

A few knowing nods went around the group; some remembered her. Others smiled at the nostalgia in my voice.

"I had this ridiculous crush on her," I admitted with a laugh. "But I never really got the courage to say anything. Anyway, that day, I figured I'd finally tell her, you know, something small, like, maybe, how nice it was to know her. Nothing dramatic." My friends burst out laughing, a few nudging me in the ribs. "That's your romantic story?" Ravi teased, shaking his head. "Did you ever get to talk to her in your lifetime?"

"Hey, not all romance needs grand gestures," I retorted with a wink. "Sometimes it's just a smile."

The group laughed again, and Ravi teased "Have you ever seen a romantic couple in school unlike your story?" I answered. "Indeed, Yes I did."

My lips are sealed

It was a regular school day, just like any other, but what happened after the final bell rang is something I'll never forget. The hallways were slowly emptying as students packed their bags and headed home, but I lingered, as I often did, chatting with friends and savoring the last moments before the day officially ended.

Imran and Rebecca, two of my closest friends, were acting a bit strange that day — whispering to each other, exchanging glances that were more intense than usual. They were always close, but something about that day felt different, almost electric. As the classrooms emptied and the school quieted, Imran and Rebecca walked out and surprisingly approached me with a request that caught me off guard.

Imran was the kind of guy who could make both academics and sports seem effortless. Famously known for his sharp mind in the classroom, he was equally mindful on the cricket field as a wicket-keeper who defied expectations. A bit on the heavier side, but quick on his feet and always alert, he proved that agility and intellect could go hand-in-hand. His reputation as both a bright student and a formidable sportsman made him stand out in our batch.

Rebecca, one of my closest friends, was known for her brilliance in studies too. She had a sharp wit that could make anyone laugh, but she wasn't one who wouldn't get a little nasty if the situation demanded. Her humor and intelligence made her stand out, and she was the kind of person who could keep you on your toes while making you enjoy every moment in her company." "Can you keep a secret?" Imran asked, his voice hushed.

"Of course," I replied, curious and intrigued.

"We need you to come with us," Rebecca added, her voice barely above a whisper.

The three of us made our way to our classroom again, now empty and silent, with the late afternoon sun casting long shadows through the windows. The atmosphere was tense, and my heart raced as I followed them inside, wondering what could be so important that they needed my presence.

Once inside, they closed the door behind us. The classroom, usually filled with the chatter of students, was now eerily quiet. I watched as Imran and Rebecca exchanged a nervous glance, and before I could ask what was going on, it happened.

They learned in towards each other, and in a moment that felt both surreal and inevitable, locked their lips in a passionate kiss. It was a long and wet kiss, one that held a world of meaning, the transition from childhood to something more complex, more mature. I stood there, the sole witness to this private moment, feeling a mix of emotions — surprise, awkwardness, and a strange sense of honor that they trusted me enough to be there.

When they finally pulled away, they both looked at me, searching for a reaction. I managed a smile, still processing what I had just witnessed.

"Don't tell anyone, okay?" Rebecca said, her cheeks flushed.

"Your secret's safe with me," I assured them, knowing that this was one story I would keep to myself — for a while, at least.

We left the classroom together, the silence now replaced with nervous laughter and a sense of something shared between us. As we walked out of the school, the world outside seemed unchanged, but for the three of us, something had shifted.

That day, the three of us walked away with a memory that would stay with us forever — a memory of friendship, trust, and the simple, unforgettable experience of growing up.

The magical tap water

After exchanging pleasantries with old friends and reminiscing about the past, my eyes caught sight of something that pulled me closer — the old tap by the playground. I remember how, back in the day, it was our sanctuary. The scorching summer heat would drive us there, cupping our hands to drink its cool water. It wasn't just water back then; it was life itself — refreshing, pure, and somehow magical.

Curious and nostalgic, I approached the tap. A slight hesitation crept in. I'd heard talk of how tap water everywhere these days was contaminated, no longer as pristine as before. But I couldn't resist. I turned the rusty handle, and the familiar gurgling sound returned, bringing with it a flood of emotions. Slowly, I cupped my hands and took a sip.

The taste was different now, slightly metallic, but as it rolled over my tongue, something profound stirred within me. It wasn't the taste of the water that mattered, but the memories it carried. I closed my eyes, remembering those endless afternoons with friends, the banter, and the races to the tap after a heated game of cricket. We used to joke that this water kept us strong, made us invincible.

In the age of overpriced bottled water, filtered for perfection, this tap water was priceless — not for its purity but for its essence. It wasn't just free in the literal sense; it was freedom. The mineral water of today, with its glossy labels and lofty promises, could never match the soul of this simple tap.

As I drank, I knew that time had changed the world, but not the connection we shared with this place. The tap, despite its wear, was still a reminder of simpler times. It kept us alive back then — not just in body, but in spirit. Today, it did the same.

I smiled, knowing that no amount of contamination could ever taint the magic that this tap held in my heart.

Opening Scene
The Grand Reunion Lunch

Venue: The Springs Hotel

The warm afternoon sun filtered through the tall glass windows of the hotel's banquet hall, casting golden streaks across the sleek marble floor. Laughter, chatter, and the clinking of glasses filled the air, blending with soft instrumental music playing in the background. A long, elegantly set table awaited the class, its white linen adorned with fresh flowers, glasses, and menus featuring a buffet of mouthwatering dishes.

I entered the hotel lobby, glancing at my reflection in the polished mirrors. I ran a hand through my hair, smiling nervously. The excitement from the classroom expedition still lingered, but this — this lunch — was the moment we all had been anticipating.

"Look at you, Mr. Popular!" Tanya teased, nudging me playfully from behind. Her eyes sparkled with amusement as she held her arm. "I swear, you're acting like a teenager again."

"I can't help it," I laughed, glancing toward the hall.... it's been so long."

Arshad raised an eyebrow, his smirk widening. "Still thinking about her, huh?" he held me nearer with his handshake.

I was a bit shocked when I noticed his hand, as it still had the old bruises, the kind I had seen during our school days.

It was a kind of trend in the past, when words alone couldn't capture the intensity of our love, some boys wrote letters in their blood, showing their devotion for their beloved. And when those love stories ended, they marked their heartbreak by stubbing burning cigarettes on their knuckles, a painful reminder of the ones they once cherished. All of a sudden, a moment from my past came flooding back.

Look who chickened out

It was in the early '90s, a time when writing love letters in blood was in vogue. Maybe we had seen someone do it in a Hindi movie and then heard about some seniors doing it and now we had come of age ourselves. Sam, one of my closest friends, had already penned several letters soaked in his blood to his girlfriend. Arshad was in another league. He would stub a lit cigarette into his knuckles in frustration whenever a breakup was looming.

I admired their dedication, if one could call it that. Every time they discussed their blood-written letters, I felt a strange kind of peer pressure. Like they had all passed the greatest test of love while I was still found missing in that department. Couldn't I even bring myself to shed some blood for love? One day, Sam came over and flaunted yet another love notes, smeared in red, a testament to his undying devotion. "This is how you show her you really care," he said with a smirk. Arshad nodded in agreement, shaking his bandaged hand from his latest cigarette burn, as if he were a battle-worn soldier of love.

Determined not to be outdone, I decided I had to step up my game. One evening, the last day of November, I decided it would be my "red letter day". I grabbed a pin, pricked my finger, and waited for the blood to ooze out. There was a small trickle of blood but it hurt. A lot. How on earth were these guys doing this? I couldn't bear to push the pin deeper, let alone enough to fill a whole page with blood. Frustrated, I stared at my barely red finger and my white paper, as clean as my conscience.

Then, in a moment of sheer genius — or stupidity — I had an idea. Did it really have to be my blood, I asked myself. Why not someone else's, or rather, something else's?

The next day, I was at the chicken shop. The butcher couldn't believe what I was saying when I asked for some chicken blood. He looked like I had lost my mind, but I didn't care. I had a mission to complete. Armed with the tiny vial of blood and a pen, I poured my feelings onto a page. I folded the letter carefully, feeling proud of my creative problem-solving.

That evening, I met Sam and Arshad again and I couldn't wait to boast that I now had my own blood letter. "See? I finally did it!" I announced, waving the letter in front of their faces.

Sam gave me a sly smile. "Not bad, man. You're finally one of us."

But Arshad, ever the skeptic, raised an eyebrow. "From which part of your body did you draw this blood?"

"Fingers," I replied quickly, holding up my hand with pride.

Arshad leaned in, inspecting my fingers like any member of my old detective agency group DRDA (Diamond Rodney Detective Agency) would. He twisted my hand this way and that, trying to find where exactly I had drawn the blood from.

"Hold on," he said, narrowing his eyes, "there's not a single mark on your fingers."

"Uh… I'm a fast healer," I stammered, feeling beads of sweat forming on my forehead.

"Fast healer, my foot," Arshad laughed, crossing his arms. "Show us where you pricked yourself."

Sam was watching with interest now, clearly smelling something fishy — or, in this case, chicken-y. I squirmed under their gaze, trying to maintain my cool, but it was no use. Finally, Arshad gave me a look that made me burst out laughing.

"Tell us the truth, or I'll check every inch of your body for wounds."

I gave up.

"Okay, okay!" I blurted out, throwing my hands up in surrender. "It's chicken blood!"

For a moment, there was silence. Sam and Arshad just stared at me, blinking, processing what they had just heard.

And then they lost it.

They burst out laughing so hard that Sam fell off the bench. Arshad clutched his stomach, tears streaming down his face. "CHICKEN BLOOD?! Are you serious?" he howled. "You went to a butcher for THIS?"

I tried to defend myself. "It looks the same, doesn't it? And it doesn't hurt!"

But there was no stopping them. Every time one of them tried to calm down, the other would start laughing again. It was contagious. Soon, I couldn't help but join in, the absurdity of the situation hitting me all at once. I had really gone to a chicken shop, thinking this would be my way of proving my worth in the bizarre world of blood love letters.

From that day on, I was known as "Chicken Boy." No matter what I did, Sam and Arshad never let me live it down. But honestly, I didn't mind. After all, in the grand scheme of things, it was a lot better than injuring my fingers for love.

And who knows, maybe someday my girlfriend would appreciate that I chose chicken blood over my own. If nothing else, at least she'd know I had a good sense of humor.

Back to the present

I reacted surprisingly, “Arshad it’s still visible even after all these years”.

He reacted immediately, “Let it go… answer me first what I asked? Still thinking of her.”

I chuckled, shaking my head, but before he could respond, I interrupted “Not here again”

As if on cue, familiar faces from my school days began to trickle in. I felt a knot of nostalgia tighten in my chest as I recognized some of my old classmates. There was John, who hadn’t changed much — well, except for the graying hair and slightly thinner waistline. He waved, catching my attention. His broad grin was the same as ever.

Suddenly, the room seemed to hum with energy, conversations overlapping as old friends reunited, exchanged jokes, and reminisced about the morning tour through their old classrooms. Memories of pranks, exams, sports days, and school trips came rushing back, filling the space between them.

Then, far from across the room, I spotted her sitting at a corner. “Sana”, my obsession in school.

She was sitting near the buffet table, chatting with a group of our old classmates, her laughter distinct and clear, sending a jolt of familiarity. My heart raced for a second, as memories of stolen glances and unspoken words flashed in my mind.

Meera noticed my gaze, and with a knowing smile yelled, “Well, Why the hell are you standing alone there, and, where is your wife?

I grinned sheepishly, but before I could say anything, Arshad intercepted me with a pat on my back. "Sameer! You look like you’ve seen a ghost!"

I laughed. “Just old memories catching up, that’s all.”

“Well, here’s to making new ones from old crushes. Do you want to talk to her,” Arshad asked, raising a glass.

“No, not at all,” I said. The room was now buzzing with life as everyone settled in for the reunion lunch.

I took a deep breath and made my way forward, the air thick with anticipation and nostalgia. The past and present collided in the air, and I couldn’t help but smile as the next chapter of this reunion began.

Arshad, our former head boy, decided to orchestrate the ultimate school reunion, promising an event that would make our glory days feel like yesterday. He went all out, securing a swanky venue, complete with gourmet food and a DJ who was booked exclusively for the boy’s night venue.

But oh, the twist! Every single lady from our batch walked in solo, as if they’d coordinated a secret “husbands, stay home” pact. Meanwhile, the men showed up in full family parade mode, wives in tow and, in some cases, a kid or two clinging to their legs like trophies of adulthood. The air was thick with the unspoken competition of whose kid could resist a tantrum the longest.

The food situation, though, was the real drama. Arshad, in his quest for culinary perfection, completely blew the budget. By dessert, he was sweating bullets, secretly calculating how many more days he’d have to keep his day job just to cover the bill. And as if that wasn’t enough, Arshad got this brainwave to go live on his phone camera, cornering people with questions like a late-night talk show host who had just found his true calling.

Then came the moment of terror. Arshad, in his live video, casually suggested that I strike up a conversation with Sana. I was paralyzed. I mumbled something awkwardly about needing to refill my drink and vanished from there. But Arshad wasn’t going to let me off the hook. He practically announced to the entire room that I was still the shy guy who couldn't muster the courage to say a word to her.

Arshad then mingled with the wives of classmates, playing the charming comedian and somehow got them all laughing at stories of their husbands' school-day antics. The whole thing felt like a sitcom where everyone but the main character is in on the joke.

The cake arrived but people were so engrossed in catching up and pulling each other's legs that it was almost forgotten. Friends who hadn't seen each other in decades reverted to their teenage selves, teasing, mocking, and reliving the good old' days as if we hadn't aged a day. The camera flashes went off like we were at a red-carpet event, with everyone grinning from ear to ear, eager to capture the moment.

Such was the feeling, people whose evening was incomplete without some liquor had not asked for even a drop. The ladies ensured that it was a sober gathering. It was, in every way, a reunion that exceeded all expectations, filled with nostalgia, laughter, and just the right amount of embarrassment to make sure we didn't forget it anytime soon.

Meera's eyes sparkled with delight as she exclaimed, "At last! After all those 'we should catch up soon' comments on Facebook, we've actually done it!"

I chuckled and replied, "Well, it only took us... what, five years of planning? Not too shabby considering our track record!"

Komal leaned in with a mock-serious expression and said, "You know, we deserve some credit here. After all those practice rounds of canceling, this was the real deal!"

Tanya quipped, "You know, we should have live-streamed this moment for our Facebook followers who still thought this reunion was just a pipe dream. It's the perfect proof that we're not just figments of their online imagination!"

"They probably still think we're just pretending to be here. They'll believe it when we post our pictures… after another five years," I said.

"We've stumbled upon the ultimate secret for successful planning: don't plan at all," said Meera. "Just show up and cross your fingers that everyone else does the same."

"Exactly," agreed Komal. "And if it fails, we'll just blame the Internet for not syncing our calendars."

"Or we could pin it on Facebook, for luring us away with those adorable cat videos every time we tried to nail down a date," quipped Tanya.

"The struggle was real, but we conquered it. Now, let's not wait another decade for the next meetup… unless, of course, we need to!" I added.

The party was on in full swing. I was standing among Meera, Tanya and Komal. I pulled out my video camera to make a quick video with the girls. "Alright, ladies, let's see those smiles! We'll preserve this moment."

Everyone struck a pose. Komal just then noticed a stain, a smudge caused by some food that had fallen on her shirt. "Hold on a second!" she exclaimed. "You can't post that!"

"Too late, I'm making it the cover photo of our reunion album," I teased.

"Oh, then do a decent job with Photoshop please. Get rid of that food stain and, also, make me look more fabulous!"

Tanya went on to add, "Oh, and don't forget to smoothen out all those wrinkles while you're at it!"

"Could you work your magic on my hair too," asked Meera. "This humidity is turning it into a wild mess!"

"Wow, you all want a full-on digital makeover! Okay, I'll turn this into a Vogue cover shoot — just let me figure out how to Photoshop videos first," I said.

They all burst out laughing and I took another shot, this time making sure the food stain was not in view.

Komal, still chuckling, warned, "You better not be serious about sharing the first one!"

With a mischievous grin, I replied, "Don't worry, Komal. I'll stash it away… as blackmail for future use."

Enter Priya — the vibrant soul of our generation. With a radiant smile that lit up every room, she charmed her way through life, excelling in public speaking, weaving words into poetry, commanding the stage in school dramas, and breathing life into her paintings. A true artist at heart, she brought warmth and creativity wherever she went.

As Priya walked in, radiating her bubbly energy, I couldn't resist poking fun at an old memory.

"Hey Priya," I grinned, leaning closer. "So, where's that guy who locked you in the classroom and left you freaking out for hours? Still keeping an eye out for him?"

Her expression first changed to shock, then exasperation and lastly she burst out laughing. The way she playfully smacked my arm indicated I might've crossed the line, but it was all in good fun.

After I'd teased her, Priya began remembering more of the story. "You know what," she said, "I actually complained to the class teacher about him afterwards. But that guy, ugh, he lied so smoothly — played innocent like a pro! And guess what? He escaped without a scratch, no punishment at all."

I laughed, picturing the whole thing. "He must've been a genius at talking his way out of trouble."

Priya shook her head, a mix of frustration and amusement in her eyes. "More like a future lawyer!"

She then made enquiries about me. "Hoping all well Sameer! How's it going? And where's your gang hiding?"

"I'm doing great, Priya. It's wonderful to see you after all these years. Hope everything's well with you too."

"I'm good, thanks! But what about your famous DRDA gang? Where are they all?"

The very mention of DRDA jolted me for a while. I recalled all the adventures.

Chapter 1

The Diamond Rodney Detective Agency

The scorching midday sun blazed through the classroom windows as Sunny, Sagar, Sandy, Sam, and I sat huddled together at our usual corner desk. We were an unlikely bunch of friends, but our love for mysteries and adventure had brought us together. Ever since we had read The Famous Five series, we had formed our own detective group — the DRDA Detective Agency.

Sunny, the calm and intelligent leader, leaned back in his chair, flipping through the pages of the latest case at hand. "Alright, team," he said, with a grin. "We've got ourselves a real challenge this time. Mrs. Rathi wants us to find out who's been stealing food from our tiffin boxes in class."

Sagar, the energetic live wire, bounced in his seat. "Finally! A real case!" His eyes gleamed with excitement. "I knew our day would come! Tiffin theft — this has 'mystery' written all over it."

Sandy, the grumpy genius of the group, crossed his arms and frowned. "Tiffin theft? Really? This better not be another false alarm. Last time we thought it was the janitor, and it turned out he was just cleaning up."

Sam and I, often there just for the fun, exchanged looks. "Let's hope this one doesn't get us in trouble," Sam muttered under his breath.

Sunny smiled. "Come on, guys. This one's different. Let's not forget our reputation is at stake. If we crack this, we'll be legends."

Chapter 2

The Investigation Begins

The next day, the investigation began. Sagar darted around during recess, pretending to be casual but observing everyone with his sharp eyes. "I'm keeping my eyes on Riaz," he whispered to the group. "He's been hanging around the canteen a lot lately."

Sunny nodded thoughtfully. "That's fine. But we can't jump to conclusions yet."

Sandy, ever the impatient one, grumbled. "He's always near food. Doesn't take a genius to make him the prime suspect."

Sunny shook his head. "We need evidence first. We can't accuse anyone without being sure."

The group trailed Riaz over the next few days, noting his habits. He was quiet, always overhearing what people said but never quite joining any conversation. Once we even caught him looking hungrily at people's tiffin boxes.

Chapter 3

The Trap

One afternoon, Sagar proposed a plan. "Let's set a trap. I'll leave my tiffin box out in the open during recess. We'll watch from a distance. If Riaz's really behind this, he won't be able to resist."

Sandy cracked his knuckles. "If he bites the bait, we catch him red-handed."

Sunny sighed, but agreed. "Alright, but let's remember — no confrontation. We just want to see if it's him."

The next day, we laid the trap. Sagar left his tiffin box on an abandoned, damaged bench outside the classroom and the DRDA team hid at vantage points from where they could see the box. Sure enough, almost in no time, Riaz was seen approaching the box, looking around nervously to ensure nobody was looking, and snatching it. The group gasped.

Chapter 4
The Confrontation

After school, we cornered Riaz near the playground. "Riaz, we know it's you," Sagar said, stepping forward. "You've been stealing our tiffin boxes."

Riaz's face turned pale. He looked at us helplessly, a look of shame and resignation on his face. There was no protest. Through his silence he seemed to be admitting to the crime.

"Why did you do it," Sagar asked.

He stammered, "I-I didn't mean to… I was just so hungry." Sandy frowned, his fists clenching. "That's no excuse! Stealing is stealing. We should tell Mrs. Rathi right now." Sagar nodded in agreement. "He's been doing this for weeks. We can't just let it slide."

But Sunny, who had been silent until now, stepped forward and placed a hand on Riaz's shoulder. "Wait." His voice was soft, understanding. "Why didn't you tell us this before, Riaz?"

Riaz's eyes welled up in tears. "I don't have lunch on most days. My dad has lost his job, and we barely have enough to eat at home. I didn't want anyone to know… I was ashamed."

Sandy opened his mouth to protest, but Sunny raised his hand. "No. We can't punish him for this. He didn't steal because he wanted to; he stole because he was desperate."

Sagar scratched his head. "But… what do we tell Mrs. Rathi then? We can't lie to her."

Sunny smiled faintly. "We won't tell a lie. We'll just… leave out a few details. Let's tell her we couldn't find the culprit. But we'll make sure Riaz doesn't have to steal anymore."

Chapter 5

A New Friend

The next day, we faced Mrs. Rathi in the classroom. She looked at us expectantly. "Well? Have you found the thief?"

Sagar shrugged. "Sorry, ma'am. We did our best, but… no luck."

Mrs. Rathi sighed, disappointed. "I expected better from the DRDA Detective Agency. But, alright. Keep trying."

As they left the classroom, Sam chuckled. "That was close."

Sunny smiled at Riaz, who was standing nearby. "Don't worry, Riaz. You're with us now."

Sandy grunted but nodded. "Yeah. Just don't steal from our tiffin boxes again."

Riaz smiled for the first time in days. "Thanks, guys. I won't. I promise."

And just like that, the DRDA Detective Agency gained a new friend, not through punishment or justice, but through understanding and compassion. It wasn't the kind of ending we were used to, but it was an ending we were proud of.

Sagar slapped Riaz on the back. "Come on, Riaz! Let's get you a proper lunch. Our treat."

Sunny grinned. "The DRDA's first case is officially closed. Onto the next one, team?"

And with that, we laughed, our bond stronger than ever.

Chapter 6

The Missing Ring

The Diamond Rodney Detective Agency was the pride of our boys, fueled by our obsession with Sherlock Holmes tales, magnifying glasses, and our makeshift detective badges made from old bottle caps. Sunny, the leader, declared the next mission: "We are going to solve the Case of the Missing Ring!" The victim was a classmate, Priya, whose precious silver ring had mysteriously vanished during class. Naturally, the detectives felt destiny was calling.

The agency, which consisted of Sunny, Sandy, Sam, Sagar, and a few other boys — including me — sprang into action. Armed with a compass, a half-eaten biscuit (for emergencies), and a notebook full of dramatic scribbles, we made our way to the crime scene: the classroom.

"Alright, boys!" Sunny declared, standing on a chair as though it were his personal soapbox. "We need to inspect every inch of this room!"

Sandy, ever the skeptic, looked around suspiciously, tapping his chin like an expert detective, though he mostly copied Sherlock's expressions from the TV show. "I suspect foul play," he murmured dramatically, although no one was sure what that meant.

Sandy, who had somehow acquired a large magnifying glass, was busy crawling under the desks, looking for clues that weren't there. "There's a hairpin! A button! A chewed-up pencil! Everything but the ring!" he reported, his voice echoing from beneath a table.

Sagar, the quiet one but the one who knew the most about all the detective jargon, whispered, "I sense something's afoot." Everyone stopped, excited by his cryptic comment.

"Yes!" Sunny yelled. "Afoot!"

Suddenly, in our investigative frenzy, we noticed something strange happening under one of the desks. A pair of feet were moving suspiciously… back and forth, back and forth. Sandy, ever the diligent observer, crawled closer, his magnifying glass practically glued to the floor. He squinted and shouted, "Guys! There's something happening over here!"

The group rushed over, surrounding the desk. And there it was — two pairs of feet, rubbing against each other in a peculiar, rhythmic dance. The detectives exchanged confused glances, unsure whether this was a clue or a scene from some alien ritual.

Sunny's voice dropped to a whisper, "This… this must be some kind of secret code!"

Sandy, not quite understanding the gravity of the situation, said with wide eyes, "Maybe they're… foot spies!"

As we peeked over the desk, we realized the feet belonged to Ricky and Jenny, a teenaged couple in school. Oblivious to the drama unfolding around them, they were lost in their own world, playing a game that could only be described as "toe tango."

Sandy blurted out, "Should we… arrest them?"

Sunny, in all his seriousness, nodded solemnly. "This is a crime… against our eyes."

The couple finally noticed the boys staring at them. Jenny's face turned beet red, and Ricky tried to play it cool, pulling his foot back as though nothing happened. "Uh… hey guys, what's up?"

Sandy was still fixated on their feet. "You two… are the Foot Rubbers!" he exclaimed as though solving a great mystery.

"Foot Rubbers?" Sam asked, biting back laughter.

"Shhh," Sunny whispered. "It's their secret identity."

Before the situation could get any more awkward, the teacher entered the classroom, causing everyone to scatter like marbles on a slick floor. In the ensuing chaos, someone knocked over a desk, and out rolled… Priya's missing ring. It was stuck in the leg of one of the tables the whole time.

The Diamond Rodney Detective Agency had cracked their second case, albeit accidentally. They might not have uncovered a jewel thief, but they had definitely uncovered something equally scandalous. As they gathered around the now-recovered ring, Sunny proudly declared, "Another case closed."

But the rest of the group was still recovering from the revelation. "Forget the ring," Sam muttered, "we just discovered the mystery of the secret foot rubbers."

That was it about the famous DRDA who were known for their intelligence and a bonding which kept them together until time separated them.

Back to the party

The school reunion Lunch party was on in full swing. I was standing near the entrance, scanning the crowd, when suddenly, I heard a familiar voice.

"Hey! Look who's here!" Sanjay's voice boomed as he walked up with a wide grin, clapping me on the back. "Man, it's been ages!"

I grinned back, "Sanjay! Finally made it, huh?"

He looked around with a mock grimace. "Yeah, yeah, but I got to say... where's the biriyani, man? Seriously, who plans a party and forgets my favorite dish?"

I burst out laughing. The word "biriyani" triggered something in my mind — another memory. Just thinking about it had me laughing all over again.

"What's so funny?" he asked, raising an eyebrow.

"Do you remember that day in school when we had that famous spicy biriyani?"

His eyes widened, and then he too started laughing, shaking his head. "Oh man, I thought I was going to die that day!"

Biryani Bonding

Location: Biryani restaurant in the suburbs

During our school days, there was one particularly memorable day that stands out. We had just lost a cricket match and spirits were sagging. In an attempt to lift our moods, Sanjay suggested that we all head out for some mind-blowing food. But this wasn't just any normal food—it was unique. For some of us, it was our first introduction to it.

The sun was setting and wavering shadows as my friends stood at the edge of the hilltop, our cycles lined up like stallions ready to charge. The thrill of competition crackled in the air as we prepared for an adrenaline-fueled race down the winding paths of the unknown streets. At the finish line awaited our ultimate prize, a famous restaurant, rumored to serve a delicacy none of us had ever tasted except our host Sanjay—something we had fantasized about for years but never had the chance to try.

The bustling city street was alive with energy. The aroma of sizzling kebabs and fried snacks from nearby stalls filled the air, mixing with the sound of honking rickshaws and vendors shouting about fresh samosas. Our group—Sanjay, Sam, Sachin, Charlie, and I —stood outside a small, dimly lit restaurant. The flickering neon sign above the door gave the place a shady charm, the kind that promised either the best meal of our life or an unforgettable trip to the emergency room.

Sanjay, always the instigator, grinned mischievously, "Alright, boys! Brace yourselves. This place is about to knock your socks off."

I raised an eyebrow, skeptical from past experiences. "You said that last time, and we ended up with burnt Naan and what? A near-death experience, remember?"

Sachin laughed, clutching his stomach. "Yeah, no kidding. I think my intestines are still in therapy from that meal."

Sanjay waved his hands defensively. "Come on! This is different. Trust me, it's the spiciest, most happening biryani in town. No burnouts, just pure flavor."

Sam shot him a look. "Spicy? Should we be excited or terrified? I don't want to be running laps after this, Sanjay."

Sachin, ever the tough guy, puffed out his chest. "Spicy is my middle name! Keep some tissues handy, Sam. You might need them."

Sanjay leaned in with an air of mystery. "Not just delicious— legendary. It's a secret family recipe. Passed down through generations. You'll taste history in every bite."

Charlie, the eternal joker, grinned. "And what happens if we start breathing fire? Will you carry us out, Sanjay?"

Sanjay smirked, "Carry you? Ha! I'll just shoot you. Now, are we going in for it?

The decision was made. We stepped inside the dimly lit restaurant, where the scent of rich spices greeted us like a warm hug. The ceiling fan overhead creaked ominously, barely keeping up with the heat that radiated from the kitchen. A waiter slid plates of biryani onto the table, each mound of rice glowing a deep, menacing red-orange. The steam rising from the dish felt like it could set off fire alarms.

Sanjay sat back, staring at the plate of spicy biryani as if it were a personal challenge. The group had already been laughing about the absurd spice level, but Sanjay was determined. Without saying a word, he stood up, his face set with the seriousness of a gladiator about to enter the arena. We all watched, expecting him to grab some water or maybe ask for a milder dish.

Instead, to our surprise, he grabbed the hem of his shirt. In one swift motion, he pulled it out of his pants and let it hang loose. But that wasn't enough. He then loosened his waist belt with a dramatic flourish, as if preparing for the feast of a lifetime. The table erupted in laughter, but Sanjay was far from done.

I gaped. "Dude... what you are doing?!"

Sanjay, unfazed, grinned and declared theatrically, "Tonight, boys, I cast aside all limitations. For this mouthwatering biryani... I am free."

Charlie snickered, "And here I thought you were just sweating from the heat."

Laughter rippled through the room as people went back to their meals, but the tension was broken. Sanjay, still shirtless, sat back down with the confidence of a man about to wrestle a lion, or in this case, a plate of spicy biryani.

Finally, we dug in. I stared at my plate, the sheer heat radiating from it making me question every life choice that had led me to this moment. "This looks like it could start a forest fire."

Sachin, already sweating after sniffing the dish, muttered, "Forget a forest, I think my nose just surrendered."

Sam, brave but foolish, took the first bite. He coughed immediately, eyes bulging. "Oh my God... it's like eating the sun. Sanjay, what did you do to us?!"

Sachin, ever the warrior, took a bite next, tears welling up in his eyes but a grin spreading across his face. "It's like a battle… every bite is a victory. And I think I'm winning."

Charlie, already fanning her mouth, laughed between coughs. "Winning? We're all losing right now, and I'm not talking about calories!"

I gingerly took a bite, and my whole body reacted as if I'd been electrocuted. "Holy... wow. This is... intense. But it's good. Really good!"

Sanjay leaned back, smug as ever. "Told you. Best biryani in town. You'll thank me later."

Sam, guzzling water as if it were the antidote to a poison, gasped, "I'll thank you if I survive this. Is this seriously the spiciest dish they have?"

Sanjay grinned wickedly. "Nah, this is the mild version."

All of us, in unison, wide-eyed: "WHAT?!"

Sanjay laughed, "Kidding! Or am I?"

Sachin groaned, "One more plate of this, and you're buying us dessert. Preferably something that doesn't melt my insides!" Despite the overwhelming spice, we couldn't stop eating. Our faces were red, eyes watering, sweat pouring down our foreheads, but the biryani was too delicious to resist. Every bite felt like we were dancing on the edge of disaster, but the laughter and camaraderie made it all worth it.

I raised my glass, my lips still burning. "Here's to new experiences, even if they come with a side of heartburn. Thanks, Sanjay."

Sanjay, still grinning, shirtless and victorious, raised his glass. "Anytime. Just wait till I take you to my next spot!"

Sam groaned dramatically. "Oh no. Let's survive this one first."

As we stumbled out into the cool night air, gasping for relief, our bellies full, our wallets lighter, and our mouths still on fire, we knew one thing for sure: this was a night we'd never forget.

As the laughter finally subsided and the last grain of spicy biryani was consumed, we leaned back in our chairs, clutching our stomachs, both from the spice and from the sheer joy of the evening. Sweat dripped from our faces, and our shirts clung to our bodies. It felt like we had just run a marathon, but the victory was sweet—or more accurately, fiery.

Sanjay, still proudly shirtless, wiped his forehead with a napkin and smirked. "Well, boys, that was one for the books. Who's ready to settle the bill?"

Sam, half-heartedly waving his hand, looked around the table. "Yeah, sure. Let's wrap this up before my mouth bursts into flames again."

The waiter approached, presenting us with a small slip of paper. Sanjay, confident as ever, grabbed it. But the moment he looked at the total, his face froze. The smirk vanished.

Sachin, noticing the shift, leaned over. "Uh, Sanjay, why do you look like you've seen a ghost?"

Sanjay blinked, cleared his throat, and tried to stay cool. "Alright, slight hiccup, guys. The bill's a bit... higher than expected."

I glanced at him suspiciously. "How high are we talking?"

Sanjay shrugged sheepishly. "A lot higher. Apparently, those extra plates of biryani weren't exactly cheap."

Charlie leaned in, snatching the bill from Sanjay's hand. His eyes widened as he read the total. "Holy... We could've bought an entire food stall for this price!"

Sam's face paled. "You're kidding, right? How much did we eat?!"

We all started frantically checking our wallets, pockets, anywhere we might have hidden extra cash. But no matter how many crumpled notes and loose coins we gathered; it was clear—we were embarrassingly short.

"Uh... guys?" I said hesitantly. "We're about a few hundred bucks short. Like, a lot of hundreds."

The realization hit all of us at once. The joyous atmosphere disappeared, replaced by a sense of dread. We exchanged glances, unsure of what to do next. None of us had brought enough cash, as we thought Sanjay will do the needful.

Sanjay tried to keep his cool. "Alright, no need to panic. I'm sure we can work something out. I'll go talk to the owner."

He stood up, still bare-chested, and swaggered over to the owner, who stood behind the counter, watching us with mild curiosity. We all followed him like a parade of shame.

Sanjay smiled, trying to charm his way out of the situation. "Hey, sir, about the bill… small problem. You see, we, uh, don't have quite enough cash on us right now. But don't worry! We're good for it. Maybe we can, uh, pay the rest later?"

The owner, a stout man with a graying mustache, raised an eyebrow, clearly unimpressed. "No cash, no problem," he said slowly, his eyes narrowing. "But you're not leaving without settling the bill."

Sanjay swallowed. "Right. Totally understandable. We're not trying to skip out or anything, we just…"

Before Sanjay could finish, the owner glanced out the window and spotted our flashy cycles, parked proudly outside.

A slow smile spread across his face.

"You boys rode bicycles here, huh?"

We all looked at each other, unsure where this was going. "Yeah," I said cautiously. "Why?"

The owner tapped his fingers on the counter and nodded toward our bikes. "Here's the deal. You leave one of those cycles as collateral. You come back tomorrow with the money, and you get your bike back. No money, no bike. Simple." A collective groan rose from the group.

Sachin shook his head in disbelief. "You've got to be kidding me. We're leaving our bikes as collateral?"

The owner crossed his arms, unfazed. "That's the deal. Or you can wash dishes."

Sam winced. "I'd rather part with the bike."

Charlie, ever the comedian, snorted. "Well, it's official. We're mortgaging our transportation for biryani."

Finally, a cycle was mortgaged to the owner for the special biriyani.

We later scrambled to gather enough money, borrowing from each other until we could cover the cost the mix of excitement and apprehension adds to the tension and fun!

Back to the reunion

As the evening got underway our reunion lunch treat was done and over and we all exited from the venue and were pretty charged up for the final exclusive boy's night out some hours away. It was not that we didn't invite the girls but we left it to them to decide if they wished to join us.

The wild night, intoxicating wine and thumping foot tapping dance was all set to roll.

Night out: The final reunion
Location: The Springs Time 8: 30 pm

The moon hung high, casting a silvery glow over the opulent ballroom, where the air crackled with anticipation and excitement. Inside, neon lights strobed in sync with the rhythm, creating a kaleidoscope of colors that danced across the crowd.

Dressed in a sharp, tailored suit, I stood at the entrance, my eyes scanning the room with a mixture of nervousness and exhilaration. Friends I hadn't seen in two decades were everywhere — dressed in their finest, catching up, and reliving old memories.

As I stepped further into the room, I was greeted with enthusiastic applause. My old buddy Jacky was leading a group in an animated discussion about our school days, waving wildly with a drink in hand. Everyone, turned out in their resplendent best, was on the dance floor, their movements a mesmerizing blur of elegance and energy.

The DJ, perched high above the crowd, had the crowd in his grasp. With a quick flick of his wrist, he switched the track to a classic '70s famous dance song, "*Do ghoonth muhje bhi pila dey sharaabi ...*" The room erupted in cheers and everyone tried to dance. The nostalgia in the air was palpable.

This was it — the night I had been waiting for, the reunion of a lifetime, with every element perfectly aligned for an unforgettable evening.

As the night progressed, the energy only intensified. The dance floor was a sea of moving bodies, lost in the music and the moment. Friends, old and new, mingled, sharing stories and rekindling bonds, while the DJ kept the tempo high, ensuring the party never lost its momentum. It was a night of pure joy, where the past and present collided in a vibrant explosion of music, laughter, and dance. As the evening wore on, I found myself lost in a deep conversation with friends, reminiscing about the old days. The atmosphere was so charged with nostalgia that I was taken back to that unforgettable night from our last day in school.

The Khatti boys' last night out
Location – National Highway

The legendary night at the fountain began with a burst of energy so electric, it felt like even the air around us was alive. The Khatti Boys — a band of misfits turned brothers for life — assembled at their famous cherished spot near a fountain, the venue for so many of their past escapades. This was no ordinary gathering; it was a farewell to the wild, unfiltered school days, where everything seemed both possible and invincible. The crew was there in full strength: Sachin, Sam, Sanjeev, Ravi and I were there, apart from some others who were there specifically for that night. Sachin, the ace tennis player and guitar player, was more than just another member of Khatti Boys. He was the voice that could rouse us from any slumber and rally us for the next big adventure. His words carried weight, and when Sachin spoke, we listened. With a mix of sharp wit and unwavering confidence, he was our spokesperson, the one who knew how to turn a plan into a promise and a moment into a memory. Sanjeev was the quintessential back bencher who injected life into the classroom with his endless knowledge of movies and music. Known for humming the latest hits and quoting iconic movie lines, he made the most mundane school days interesting. Ravi was the quiet observer in the group, often blending into the background with an air of calm. But behind his silence lay a sharp mind and a wit that could catch anyone off guard. His rare, well-timed remarks always left people in awe and splits.

We had our bikes, our dreams, and the night spread out before us like an open map, waiting to be explored.

The last rays of the sun surrendered to the dusky purple of evening, casting long shadows that only added to the thrill. Our bikes stood in line, each polished to perfection, their chrome parts reflecting the glow of the streetlights. We revved up our engines to a growl, a promise of the chaos to come. We were modern-day cowboys, ready for our last great ride, and the city was our wild frontier.

The plan was simple: ride out to the edge of the city, a place where the roads were straight and traffic sparse, perfect for pushing our limits. We had undertaken similar rides during the grand festival of Dussehra, when the streets were alive with lights and celebrations, and everyone in the city seemed to be out on the streets, if not dancing too.

In those days, festivals weren't just a time for celebration — they epitomized the unbreakable thread that bound us together. We were more than friends; we were like family, bound by a deep-rooted unity that transcended all differences. Among the myriad festivals we shared, a few stood out for their unique warmth and tradition.

Mohit, John and Sujoy, my closest friends, played a very special role in this. Mohit, with his striking sense of humor and comic timing, was my favorite. John, the first friend I made in school, was a lively, funny character, who enjoyed pulling people's legs till they were irritated. He had a playful energy and, along with Sam and Jacky, was the heartthrob of many at St. Peterson Girls' School.

Sujoy was a friend in need. Rich and elegant, he possessed a heart of gold, standing out not just for his wealth but also for his character. His unwavering support was a source of strength for anyone going through a tough time. Whether it was late at night or anytime of the day anyone despaired, Sujoy would always be by his friend's side without hesitation.

During Eid, I would invite everyone over, and together, we'd sit around the table enjoying the biryani, which had become another symbol of our unity. Plates filled to the brim, we would joke, eat, and celebrate. No force on earth could divide us, we believed.

And during Ganesh Puja, Mohit would invite us all to his house. It was more than just a ritual; it was an unspoken tradition that none of us would miss. Mohit's family would prepare a grand feast — delicious puris, spiced potato curry, and desserts that had us coming back for more. Fragrance from the burning incense mixed with the aroma from the food to create magic in our minds and bellies. We didn't just sit and eat; we celebrated the essence of friendship, all of us under one roof, laughing, sharing stories, and feeling at home in each other's company.

The highlight of the year was the vibrant nights during Dussehra in Cuttack. Sujoy, our quiet friend, would invite us to his family's bungalow, where the tables groaned under the weight of mouth-watering Bengali dishes. The richness of the food was rivaled only by the richness of our bond. After dinner, we'd venture out on Cuttack's lit-up streets, alive with music, dance, and celebration. Year after year during Dussehra, Cuttack transformed itself into a wonderland of lights, sounds and aromas. It was the perfect time to explore the city, laughing and reveling in the festival's magic, knowing these were the moments that would remain etched in our minds forever.

But the year of celebrations wasn't over till we had attended John and his family's Christmas bash. The warmth of the holiday spirit was matched only by the incredible hospitality John's family extended to everyone who walked through their door. His mother was known for the delicious and sumptuous festival dishes she prepared, especially the Christmas cake, while his father made sure there was laughter and joy in abundance. At John's house we friends felt at ease sharing our stories, food, and the Christmas spirit. The tradition of love and togetherness made each of our festivals unforgettable.

In those days, religion or background did not impact our friendship and equations. We were simple humans, connected by the purest form of togetherness. It was an era where the only thing that mattered was our bond, and that was the only religion we needed. The festivals became a way for us to celebrate not just the occasions themselves, but the friendship that had grown deeper with each passing year. There was no religious distinction, no barrier among us. It was as if we spoke the same language — which could be called love, friendship and/or unity.

And that night was the last time we would celebrate that camaraderie. Since life as we knew it was on the verge of changing forever as we moved on in life.

Sam, ever the daredevil, kicked off the madness with a grin on his face as he twisted his accelerator full throttle. His mean machine roared to life and shot off, like it had just been fired from a cannon. Behind him the others followed, wheels after wheels, zooming past, trying to lead the race, show the way.

We were scattered here and there on the streets, some still running handle to handle while trying to edge past, others very close, but Sam was way ahead, powered as much by his attitude as his mean machine. He was clearly in a state of mind that was different from any of ours that day. If it had been day, we would clearly have seen some rubber mark his tires stamped on the road, leaving his **Bullet's** signature, an autograph given without anyone asking for it.

But he wasn't content with just that. He had more plans. He leaned back suddenly, letting one of his hands leave the handlebar to run his fingers through his unruly hair. "Look, man! No hands!" he hollered, his laughter trailing behind him like a comet. The city lights flashed on his face, a kaleidoscope of reckless joy.

Sanjeev, his unfortunate pillion rider, was clutching at Sam's waist like it were his lifeline. His eyes were wide, darting between the speeding road and Sam's carefree display. "Help! Someone, please! He's driving like we're on a suicide mission!" he screamed, his voice drowned out by the roar of the bikes and the swoosh of the wind. If Sam heard him, he didn't show it; he just revved up further, slicing through the air like an arrow.

Behind them, I was piloting my own ride, with Sachin sprawled lazily behind me. Sachin, who had a drink too many before we started, now swayed in a state of perfect, drunken equilibrium. He leaned forward, his breath warm and reeking of alcohol, and whispered into my ears, "Sam should really slow down, don't you think?" His tone was calm, almost philosophical, as if the thought had just occurred to him on a serene afternoon rather than in the middle of a midnight race.

The road unfolded before us, stretching into the darkness like a ribbon of dreams. The thrill of speed pumped in our veins, making our shouts and laughter louder, our grins wider. And then came the moment that cemented that night into our system forever.

Dara, who had a penchant for theatrics, suddenly zoomed past all of us, even overtaking Sam. And then all of a sudden, his bike screeched to a halt. He jumped off and barked, "How many push-ups can you do, huh?" Before anyone even understood what he was driving at, he came down on all fours on the road, palms flat against the warm asphalt, and began doing dips. “One, two, three” — his voice a challenge to the night. The others went with the flow. Bike after bike screeched to a halt as more members joined in this impromptu push-up contest.

"Fifty, bro!" shouted Sachin, his eyes gleaming under the streetlights. Sanjeev laughed so hard he nearly fell off his bike, slapping Sam on the back. Ravi, the quietest of the lot, surprised everyone by jumping in and going well past 50, his face set in serious concentration.

After a short break, the bikes roared to life again, leaving behind shocked yells from late-night drivers who could hardly believe what they were seeing. We were the Khatti Boys, taking one last, wild stand before the future pulled us apart, sending us to different colleges, cities, and destinies. But that night, with the scent of burnt rubber in the air and the echo of our laughter bouncing off silent buildings, we were untouchable.

We rode side by side, engines purring like satisfied cats, and not a word was needed. We had our stories, and we knew we’d be talking about this night for the rest of our lives.

And as I glanced over my shoulder at the faces of my friends, wild and worn-out, I knew the truth: legends might fade, but this night, this feeling, was ours forever.

Unforgettable slaps
Location: Café at the countryside

We all halted at the countryside cafe for a break. The evening was electric with anticipation. The last day of school had been a whirlwind of emotions, but the night out with my best friend Sam had promised to be an unforgettable crescendo. Sam was the epitome of charisma — handsome, brilliant, and a Casanova. He was the kind of guy who could light up a room and leave everyone in awe. But that night, beneath the glitter of celebration, a storm was brewing.

We had gathered at our favorite hangout, the dimly lit cafe where laughter and chatter drowned out the rest of the world. The air was thick with the scent of spilled drinks and the hum of high spirits. Sam, ever the life of any party, was in full swing, his laughter ringing out above the clamor. But as the night wore on, the drinks flowed more freely, and Sam's demeanor began to change.

In a haze of intoxication, Sam leaned in, his eyes gleaming with a mix of mischief and fury. He told me a story that seemed almost too outrageous to believe, but the intensity in his voice made it clear he was dead serious.

“Remember Mr. Thompson?” he began, his voice slurring slightly. “That old sports teacher who made our lives a living hell? I’ll never forget that day. It all started with a heated argument which was baseless. He humiliated me in front of the entire class — slapped me back-to-back, one after another. Each slap was a thunderclap of disgrace, echoing through the classroom as he pummeled me with his wrath.”

I could hardly believe what I was hearing. Mr. Thompson was known for his strictness, but those slaps? That was beyond anything I could imagine. Sam’s face was a mix of pain and rage as he continued.

“He was relentless,” Sam said, his voice growing more fervent. “Each slap was like a badge of dishonor, each hit a mark of his cruelty. I vowed then and there that one day, I would make him pay for his injustice. I would find a way to get back at him, no matter what it took."

His words were fiery, his eyes blazing with a dangerous determination. I could see the depth of his anger, how it had simmered over the years. He was a man on a mission, driven by a promise he made to himself in the darkest hour of his school days.

Years passed, and life moved on, but the shadow of that night loomed large. When the school reunion was announced, there was a palpable buzz of excitement. But as the day approached, it became clear that Sam was nowhere to be found. His absence was a gaping hole in the celebration.

I felt a pang of sadness as I looked around the room, searching for him among the familiar faces. Sam was more than just a friend; he was a brother in arms, a kindred spirit with a heart of gold and a strength that had always been my anchor.

As the reunion progressed, the room was filled with chatter and memories, but without Sam, it felt incomplete. The stories of the past seemed to echo in the empty space he left behind.

Sam had promised to return one day, to settle the score with Mr. Thompson. But on this night, it was his absence that spoke the loudest.

In the end, Sam's tale was a testament to the burning fires of revenge and the bonds of friendship that outlast time and distance. And though he was not there with us in the reunion his spirit lingered, a reminder of the loyalty and strength that had once defined him.

But the worst memory of that unforgettable night apart from Sam's tale was yet to happen.

The Face-off

Location – Countryside restaurant Time 12:00 midnight

That night was electric with a wild sense of freedom, a freedom that came from knowing it was our last day of school. The air was thick with excitement as close friends Sachin & Ronnie, and our group of friends tore through the dimly lit countryside roads on roaring bikes, laughing, shouting, and daring each other to push the limits. They were drunk, their heads swimming in alcohol and adrenaline, a cocktail of chaos that only made their triple bike rides more dangerous, more exhilarating.

We arrived at a rundown restaurant tucked away in the woods, its neon sign flickering weakly, but to us, it felt like the gateway to a night we would never forget. Sachin and Ronnie stumbled in with the others, their arms slung over each other's shoulders, the best of friends. At least, until the conversation veered off course.

"Remember Ria?" Sachin said suddenly, his eyes half-closed with intoxication but full of an unmistakable fondness.

Ronnie's ears perked up. "Ria from WIFI club?"

"Yeah, man," Sachin grinned. "I've been in love with her and I am just too scared to tell her."

The table went quiet. The music faded into the background; the distant hum of the restaurant almost drowned out by the tension that suddenly filled the room. Ronnie's expression darkened, and for a second, he looked at Sachin like he failed to recognize him. For a moment I was taken aback by the very mention of Ria the heartthrob of the WIFI club. The memories started flooding in about that unforgettable night at the famous WIFI club, the talk of the town.

WIFI club from another era

This happened long before you saw it at a cinema hall near you. Because even before the movie was released, the city had its own Rajput School and Model School rolled into one, called Centurion, and its own Queen's College, called St Peterson. And their rivalry and competition were legendary. Be it studies, or sports, or arts and culture, they all believed that only the best can win. Or, in other words, *Jo Jeeta Wohi Sikandar*.

The spotlight beamed onto the stage as the boys from Centurion School prepared to unleash their secret weapon—a live performance from the famous chartbuster The Final Countdown. Sachin, the lead guitarist, stood poised with his fingers lightly brushing the strings of his electric guitar. To his right, my master synthesizer, fiddled with knobs and switches, conjuring an array of ethereal sounds. At the center, Mahesh, the lead vocalist, was a picture of calm before the storm. Mahesh had a magical voice and he was our leading singer of that evening.

The girls of St. Peterson, sitting on the other side of the club, whispered among themselves, trying to hide their excitement behind teasing smiles. There was palpable excitement among the girls from St. Peterson. Among them sat Ria, the most sought-after girl, looking nonchalant but clearly intrigued.

As the first notes of the intro to a popular song Mere rang mein rangne wali from the Salman Khan Movie Maine Pyar Kiya the Indian version of The Final Countdown boomed from the speakers, a wave of excitement swept through the crowd.

My fingers danced on the keys, creating an eerie yet exhilarating build-up. Sachin followed with a power chord that reverberated through the room, his guitar screaming to life. And then, Mahesh's voice soared—strong and pitch-perfect, carrying the iconic chorus with ease.

The crowd erupted in applause, with the girls of St. Peterson bobbing their heads and clapping along. A few of them even tried to act unimpressed, but it was clear they were falling under the spell. Sachin shredded through his solo with confidence, the riffs cutting through the air like lightning, while my synthesizer lifted the entire performance into an otherworldly crescendo.

The performance ended in a storm of applause and cheers. The boys from Centurion had done it—they had won over the crowd, and more importantly, they had won over the girls. But the night wasn't over yet.

The MC's voice boomed through the mic, "And now, to steal the stage, we have St. Peterson's very own Ria!" A murmur rippled through the club as the boys leaned forward with anticipation.

Ria stepped onto the stage, the lights catching the shimmer of her outfit as the opening beats of a famous actress Madhuri Dixit chartbuster movie Tezaab number, Ek Do Teen, filled the room. She moved with grace, each step perfectly choreographed, her expressions sharp and captivating. The excitement in the room was explosive.

The boys from Centurion watched in awe, their earlier swagger replaced by sheer admiration. Ria's dance moves were flawless—fluid, yet powerful—and with every spin and gesture, she captivated the audience.

Among the boys, one particular friend stood frozen, his heart pounding in sync with the music. He had heard of Ria's charm, but nothing had prepared him for this. The way she moved, the energy she brought to the stage—it was as if the world had tilted, and he was now orbiting around her. He watched, mesmerized, unable to tear his eyes away.

As the song reached its climax, Ria executed her final twirl and struck a dramatic pose. The crowd went wild, screaming her name like they had Madhuri's, or Mohini's, in the movie. That was the moment when Ria had not only conquered the stage but also won over the boys of Centurion, particularly Sachin.

The party roared on, but for him, everything else was a blur. Sam, Mahesh, and I teased him mercilessly, recognizing the look on his face—a look of love-struck wonder. "Looks like you've met your match, buddy," Sam grinned, nudging him.

He couldn't help but smile, his eyes still following Ria as she rejoined her friends. "I think I've fallen in love," he whispered, mostly to himself. But in the chaos of that thrilling night, under the lights of the WIFI Club, something had sparked—a moment he would never forget.

As the music thumped and the crowd danced late into the night, it was clear that this face-off between Centurion and St. Peterson was not just a contest of talent. It was a celebration of youth, of first crushes, of friendships forged in the heat of competition, and of memories that would linger long after the music stopped. Love was in the air.

Back to the Face-off

The battle was still ongoing.

"Wait... you love Ria?" Ronnie's voice was thick, his words slurred but the meaning sharp.

Sachin, too drunk to notice the shift, nodded eagerly "Yeah, man. I've been crazy about her since the first time w met at the club. She's... I mean, you know how she is-gorgeous, smart. A dream."

Ronnie's face hardened; his fists clenched. "She's not j a dream to you. I love her too."

Sachin blinked, the alcohol clouding his mind not q enough to process the weight of Ronnie's words. "What?

unspoken emotions that had been bubbling beneath the surface for far too long.

Finally, as the confrontation reached its peak, Sachin threw his hands up. "This is pointless! You know what, Ronnie? If you think you're the one for her, go ahead. I don't care anymore."

But the bitterness in his voice betrayed his words. He cared.

Ronnie, visibly shaken, didn't respond. The group fell into an awkward, heavy silence. The night, once filled with laughter and reckless joy, now felt hollow, like a balloon deflating slowly under the weight of crushed hopes and fractured friendships.

Eventually we all left the restaurant, no longer as one group, but as two factions, silently heading back on our bikes into the dark countryside. What was supposed to be our last wild night together ended in shattered bonds and unspoken pain, all because of Ria—a girl who might never know the heartbreak she had unknowingly caused.

As the sun began to rise, casting a golden light over the landscape, it felt like a bittersweet reminder that nothing lasts forever, even the Friendship which was short-lived. That night ended soon and on the other hand it was just the beginning of our foray into another world known as "The College life" where we all stepped in, super excited but the group was no more the same, as we all stood a bit far away divided and scattered like a pack of cards.

Back to the present: Closing reunion scene

It was a night that would be remembered as long as there were still people to tell the tale. The laughter slowly faded, replaced by the soft murmur of farewells. Hugs were exchanged, hands lingered in reluctant parting, and eyes shimmered with a quiet understanding of time's passage. Standing together one last time, we promised — amid smiles and playful jabs — to meet again, sooner this time.

Finally, the inevitable came. Cars and bikes were started, engines hummed to life, and one by one, the friends began to pull away. I stood alone watching the taillights disappear in the dark. With a final glance at the empty parking lot, I whispered to himself, "Until next time, my friends." And with that, I turned towards the warmth of my family, ready to carry the memory of this night forward, like a hidden treasure buried deep in my heart. Finally, the reunion came to an end and I was all set to board the next flight, back to Dubai.

Dubai calls

Location: Airport

After ten days of a whirlwind journey through two states, exhaustion weighed heavily on me as I stood at the bustling International Terminal. The last day in Mumbai had been a blur — hours spent navigating crowded streets, shopping bags filled to the brim, and a hangover from a late-night celebration that still lingered. All I wanted now was to board the plane, close my eyes, and wake up in Dubai, my home, where the comfort of familiarity awaited.

As the plane ascended into the sky, I finally began to relax. My wife, Sofia, and our two little wonders were already fast asleep beside me, their faces peaceful despite the chaos of the past few days. The hum of the engines, the rhythmic sway of the flight — it all lulled me into a sense of calm. But just as sleep began to take hold, the plane shuddered violently, tossed by turbulent clouds. My heart raced, jolted awake by the sudden surge of anxiety. The next twenty minutes felt like an eternity, the turbulence shaking not just the plane, but my nerves as well. Sofia woke up, gently holding my hand, offering the solace I needed in that moment. She asked, "How was the reunion? In short, did you meet all your teachers and friends?"

I paused for a moment, reflecting. “Yes, almost all,” I replied, “except for one — Mr. Gonzales, the computer teacher who was missing”

“Why?” she asked, curious.

I smiled, feeling a wave of old memories rise within me. It was time to share a story I had kept to myself for so long.

The Forbidden dream

Back in the early ‘90s, when computers were the stuff of legends — shiny, mysterious machines that hummed like they held the secrets of the universe — I stood at the threshold of the great divide. On one side, the blessed, chosen few who had scored over 80% had been able to study computer science. On the other side… well, my friends and I, had not been that lucky.

Our school had a special room for computers, which might as well have been made of gold. To even get a glance of that air-conditioned sanctuary, you had to score top marks. And there was only one gatekeeper to this tech wonderland: Mr. Gonzales, our computer science teacher, a man who looked like he was born wearing a tie and glasses. But only ten among us and the teacher who taught computer science, Mr. Gonzales, had access to this room. The rest of us studied commerce.

The first time I asked him to let me take computers as a subject, he gave me a look that could freeze a volcano. "You?" he said, raising an eyebrow so high I thought it might fly off his face. “Your marks… they are not enough.” The way he said it, I’d think I was asking for the password to a secret government database.

“But sir,” I stammered, “I really want to learn about computers! I’ll work hard it’s my fascination, my dream. Please give me one chance.”

“Computer is not for everyone,” he said, his voice as cold as the air-conditioned room behind him. "Only the top students. You should focus on other subjects."

Other subjects? The ones where I spent most of my time doodling in the back of my notebook? No, this was a grave injustice. I couldn’t even see the computers. They kept that room sealed tighter than the principal’s office on exam day.

It wasn’t just about the subject. It was about the idea of computers, those glowing monitors that flickered with dreams. All I ever saw was the faint blue light spilling out whenever someone left the door ajar. It was like peeking into a forbidden place and being told, “Sorry, this wardrobe is only for chosen ones.”

I couldn’t take this discrimination any more.

So, one day, I snapped. I marched right up to Mr. Gonzales, chest puffed out like I was about to take on a heavyweight champion. “Mr. Gonzales,” I said, my voice shaking slightly but my resolve stronger than ever. “It’s unfair that you didn’t let me study computers. Just because I didn’t get the highest marks doesn’t mean I can’t learn!”

He looked at me with the same old arrogant stare, but I wasn’t backing down.

“Marks aren’t everything!” I declared. “One day, every household will have a computer! Even the kids… kids won’t even care about your precious computer room. They’ll treat these machines like toys, like playthings! And they will never require your permission to touch one!”

Mr. Gonzales’s face didn’t change, but I could sense a slight twitch in his eye. I had gotten under his skin.

"That day," he said, "is far, far away boy. For now, you need to focus on what you can do, not what you can't."

The cold war had begun. For weeks, I avoided him, silently fuming as the "elite" class trooped past me to their computer lessons, laughing and chatting as if they were on their way to a secret club. Meanwhile, I was stuck with subjects like geography, wondering if knowing the capital of Zimbabwe would ever give me the same thrill as booting up a computer.

But I had made my curse. Every day, I whispered to myself, "One day… one day, everyone will have a computer!" It became my mantra.

Years later, when I finally got my hands on a PC, the first thing I did was laugh. It wasn't the magical machine I'd imagined. The screen was bulky, the mouse had a ball in it, and getting it to connect to the internet felt like trying to talk to aliens. But it was mine. And more importantly, it was everywhere—in homes, in schools, in cafes. Even kids could operate them better than most adults.

"Once, only students who scored 80 percent and above were allowed to study computer science. Today, the situation has reversed—students take up computer science to score top marks."

I like to imagine Mr. Gonzales sitting somewhere in his old classroom, watching as every student brings their own laptop to school. Kids with tablets, smartphones, and devices he never thought possible, treating them like the toys I had once predicted.

And I wonder… does he remember me? Does he remember the kid who cursed him that day?

Or is he too busy trying to figure out how to get the Wi-Fi working?

At last, I said, "It's today because of only computer and technology that I could make it to the reunion with my school friends today."

Back to the flight

When the plane finally stabilized, I gazed out of the window at the sea below, its shimmering surface reminding me of Jumeirah Beach in Dubai. The memories of the trip began to fade, replaced by a yearning for home. As I drifted into a light sleep, the flight seemed to pass in an instant, interrupted only by the announcement that we were about to land in Dubai. It felt too soon, almost as if time had slipped through my fingers while I was lost in thought.

The landing was smooth, a welcome relief after the bumpy ride. As we disembarked, the weight of the journey began to lift, replaced by the simple joy of being back on familiar ground. Sofia and the kids hurried ahead, eager to reach home, while I waited impatiently for our luggage to appear on the carousel. Finally, I spotted our bags and began pulling them towards the exit, my mind already on the soft bed that awaited me.

But just as I was about to step out into the warm Dubai air, my phone buzzed insistently in the pocket. At first, I ignored it, too tired to care about any updates. But the buzzing continued, and with a sigh, I pulled out my phone, expecting nothing more than a mundane notification. Instead, I found myself staring at a name that had not crossed my mind in years — "Sana"

My breath caught in my throat as I opened the message. My hands trembled, disbelief washing over me like a cold wave. There, on my screen, was a message from her, the girl who had been a part of my life two decades ago, before the world changed, before our paths diverged. "Thought of talking to you...... thank you for your great initiative for the reunion." she messaged.

The words blurred before my eyes as my mind spiraled back through the years. Why now? Why after all this time? A flood of emotions swept over me—confusion, excitement, a

flicker of joy, but also fear. What could this mean? What did she want?
And most importantly, what did it mean for the life I had built, the family that depends on me?

I quickly glanced around, catching sight of Sofia and the kids waiting for me near the exit. Panic surged. What would they think if they knew? I couldn't let them see me like this. I mumbled an excuse about needing to use the washroom and hurried away, my heart pounding in my chest. Inside the washroom, I locked myself in a stall, desperate for privacy, and reread the message, hoping it might make more sense the second time.

But it didn't. Instead, it only raised more questions. Why hadn't she spoken to me at the reunion? What had changed in her life that made her reach out now? Was she alright? Was this some kind of closure, or was it the beginning of something I had long buried?

My mind raced with possibilities, each one more troubling than the last. I am married, with a family that I loved dearly. How could I even think of responding to her? And yet, a part of me—the part that remembered the boy I was decades ago—ached to reach out, to understand why this message had come now, after so long.

This was a moment I had dreamed of in my youth, when the pain of our parting was still fresh. But that was a lifetime ago. Now, the stakes were different, the consequences potentially devastating. I had a choice to make, and it was one of the hardest I had ever faced.

As I stood there, the phone still clutched in my hand, I felt the weight of the years between us. Time had changed everything, yet some things — some emotions — remained stubbornly the same. I could feel the pull of the past, the longing for answers, for closure. But there was also the fear of what those answers might bring, of what they might cost.

I took a deep breath, trying to steady my racing heart. This wasn't the life I had expected, but it was the life I had chosen. And now, at this crossroads, I had to decide what mattered most.

There's a pull, an invisible thread that tugs at the heart in the quietest of moments. I had long thought I'd freed myself from this thread, buried it beneath layers of time and distance, and the life I'd built. But this visit made me realize the thread was still very much there, binding me to my memories of her. After all those years, I felt it tug at my heart strings. Triggering a familiar flutter in my heart. That ache I believed was long gone.

The desire to meet her again, to hear her voice, to remember what it once was, overwhelmed me. I fought it, I really did. But some emotions refuse to die. That first love — so sweet and painful — had its own language, one that only I understood. And in the end, the heart won over reason, as it always does.

I found myself walking back. I could feel the weight of my past and present colliding, but in that moment, none of it mattered. I had succumbed to love again — an old love, a love that never really left me. I turned around and rushed toward the departures area of the airport, looking for the next flight back to India.

The airport was abuzz with the chaos of calls for boarding and rolling suitcases, but all I could hear was the pounding in my heart. The gates for the flight to India — the one that could change everything — were about to close any minute now.

"Final call for passengers..." echoed.

I broke into a sprint, weaving through the crowd, dodging travelers with an urgency I hadn't felt in years. Each step was a race against time, each breath a countdown. My mind flashed back to the past and the way things ended — unfinished.

As I hurried toward the gate, I saw a glass window in front of me, through which I could see passengers proceeding to catch their flights.

I peered through the glass, feeling helpless. One minute I thought I must go ahead, even if I didn't have a ticket. Another minute I thought maybe I was being impractical. I was lost. I decided to sit down. I looked up at the screen, to the flight schedule, my heart pounding with every passing second. It was as if the world had come to a halt, and the only thing that mattered was making it to that flight. Desperation gnawed at me. My mind raced back to memories of my friends — the ones who, in another time, would have been by my side, laughing, egging me on.

Sam would have been the first to say something, his calm voice reassuring me. But he was lost in his own world now. Jacky would have taken the next flight to meet me, if he could. The other school friends, the ones who knew me inside out, were gone — lost to time, to distance, to life itself. No one was there to help me, no one to stand by my side and pull me through.

And in that moment, the crushing weight of loneliness hit me. For the first time, I truly felt it — the absence of those who had once been the world to me. They would have made sure I sailed through this phase, laughing through the panic. But now, there was no one left to carry me through.

I stood at the terminal, my heart racing, watching the backs of passenger's fade in the distance. I started imagining that she was there, somewhere, slipping away like she had all those years ago, on the last day at school. But just like then, it was too late. A sense of helplessness engulfed me, just as it had when I was a teenager, watching her walk away on the last day of school through the gates without knowing when, or if, I'd see her again.

I was alone.

The harsh fluorescent lights bounced off the towering glass windows, casting an almost clinical brightness over the chaotic serenity. Suddenly, the sound of an engine whipped through the monotonous hum of the airport. Then, a gust of wind swept past me, cold and familiar, cutting through the warmth of the terminal's recycled air. The deep, guttural roar of a Royal Enfield Bullet echoed through the vast terminal, a sound that shouldn't have been there.

My pulse quickened. It wasn't just any engine — it was his engine. I looked up, almost afraid of what I'd see, my heart in my throat. And there he was. Suraj.

He rode into the airport on his beloved Bullet, the machine gleaming under the artificial lights like something out of a dream — or nightmare. He was dressed in the same old faded leather jacket, his hair ruffled from the wind. He looked like the Suraj I knew, but sharper somehow, more vivid, like he didn't quite belong to this world anymore. His bike wasn't just any Bullet; it was his Bullet — his "antic" Bullet, as he always called it, a machine that seemed to growl like a living beast under him.

The airport's noise dimmed as he approached, but no one seemed to notice. People walked past as if they could not see him or his bike, as if the floor wasn't trembling with his presence. But only I could see him. I could hear him. Even if the rest of the world remained oblivious.

Suraj pulled up right beside me. A whiff of gasoline and leather filled the air, and I stood frozen, my body refusing to believe what I was seeing. He kicked the stand down with that same reckless swagger of his, and swung off the bike as if nothing had changed — as if he hadn't been gone for years.

His eyes met mine, and for a split second I forgot that he wasn't supposed to be here. I even forgot that he had been dead.

"Long time no see, huh?" he said, his voice audibles over the airport din as if it was the only sound that mattered.

I couldn't speak or move. A rush of emotions came over me — grief, joy, fear, disbelief — all at the same time in a knot so tight, I could barely breathe.

Suraj smirked, that cocky grin of his that always meant trouble. "What? Cat got your tongue?" He patted the Bullet as if it were an old friend. "Thought I'd swing by and steal the show one last time."

I blinked, finally finding my voice, though it came out as barely a whisper. "You're... you're not real."

He shrugged; the movement casual, effortless. "Maybe. But here I am. You missed me, didn't you?"

A part of me wanted to laugh, cry, and scream all at once. But all I could do was stare. No one around us reacted; people passed through us like shadows, as if the roar of his bike hadn't just echoed through the entire terminal, as if a ghost wasn't standing right in front of me, larger than life.

He looked around, taking in the oblivious crowd. "They never could handle my style," he said, grinning like a mischievous kid. "Don't worry though, I'm just here for you."

He leaned against his bike, folding his arms. "Maybe I felt like you needed me. Or maybe I needed to see you. Does it matter?"

His eyes — those same eyes that had always danced with a fire no one could quite match — locked onto mine, and suddenly, it didn't matter. He was here, and for a moment, it was as if he'd never left.

Suraj's laugh broke the silence, sharp and full of life. "Still can't believe no one hears me. Weird, huh?" He revved up the engine again, and it roared in response, the sound somehow both alive and otherworldly, shaking me from my trance.

I stood frozen, the chaotic sounds of the airport fading into a dull hum around him. His heart raced as he glanced at the departure gate, where the final boarding call for the flight echoed like a haunting reminder. "What's the matter, Sameer?" Suraj's voice cut through his thoughts; concern etched across his face. "I want to catch the next flight home to be with her, Sana. The flight is about to leave, and I need your help!" My voice sounded urgent, filled with desperation.

Suraj's expression shifted, worry tightening his features. "What? For this girl?" His voice grew tense, each word punctuated with a sense of urgency. "Why? She is not meant for you! Forget her. You've wasted enough precious time after her. She never reciprocated your feelings. She never cared about you, and yet you want to be with her?"

I felt a storm of emotions rising within me — frustration, anger, but also a flicker of truth. Deep down, I knew Suraj was speaking from a place of concern. But the thought of losing Sana sent a cold wave of fear through me.

"She never understood you, Sameer! Not for this girl!" Suraj's voice rose above the din of the crowd, drawing glances from passersby. "Leave her! You have your family waiting for you at that gate — that's your life! Sofia left her home for you. It's high time you move on with your family."

"Does she love you more than Sofia does?" Suraj's voice was firm, each word a heavy weight. "Not at all. Sofia stood by you during every phase of your life like a pillar. Sana isn't worth it compared to Sofia. Step back; your world is waiting for you at that gate. Move back, reach out to them! Leave Sana; she is not the one for you!"

Suddenly, as if he had crossed an invisible line, Suraj's figure began to shimmer and fade, his face a mix of frustration and sadness. "No! Suraj!" I cried out, searching left and right for him. "Suraj, where are you?"

Then, out of nowhere, Suraj appeared on the runway, astride a roaring motorcycle, a wild look in his eyes. "Go back, Sameer! Go back to your family! Don't commit the mistake I did!" His voice was a powerful command, ringing through the whir of engines, of his Bullet and that of the India-bound aircraft as it rolled on the tarmac, and the rush of people.

Suraj waved at me, and with a swift motion he revved up his engine, the Bullet's roar echoing like thunder. He performed a daring wheelie, after which his figure became a blur. "Come back my friend!" I shouted, but the words felt powerless as Suraj sped away, the image of my best friend fading into the darkness.

With every heartbeat, the truth of Suraj's words tore through me: the love I chased was as ethereal as the wind. The sight of the airplane taking off sent a shudder through me, and for a moment I felt a profound emptiness.

As the plane vanished into the sky, I stood at the edge of my dreams and reality, torn between the echoes of an unrequited love and the steady pull of life waiting for me just beyond that gate. In the chaos, I realized it wasn't just about Sana anymore; it was about choosing myself, about understanding the value of love that was real, tangible, and steadfast.

With a deep breath, I turned my eyes from the runway, my heart heavy yet determined. I took a step towards the gate, ready to reclaim the pieces of myself I had almost lost. I was back with family, leaving the past forever.

Epilogue

As I posted my final update on Facebook, I wrote, "Reunions aren't about the past—they're about rediscovering the present with the people who helped shape it. Until next time, friends."

With that, I logged off, a sense of calm settling over me. I knew now that some things, like true friendships, last a lifetime. The beauty of school friends lies in its unique bond—they've seen you grow, they know your roots, your dreams, your flaws. Life may bring new friendships, but it's those early friends who stand the test of time. They are the ones who will always be there, in the moments that matter, no matter how far life takes you.

The phone buzzed again, cutting through the silence. My heart raced as I glanced at the screen. One name flashed: "Sana". I froze. After everything, after all this time — why now? What could possibly come next?